Great Basin Experimental Range: Annotated Bibliography

E. Durant McArthur,
Bryce A. Richardson and
Stanley G. Kitchen

 United States Department of Agriculture / Forest Service
Rocky Mountain Research Station
General Technical Report RMRS-GTR-305WWW

June 2013

McArthur, E. Durant; Richardson, Bryce A.; Kitchen, Stanley G. 2013. **Great Basin Experimental Range: Annotated bibliography**. Gen. Tech. Rep. GTR-305WWW. Fort Collins, CO: U.S. Department of Agriculture, Forest Service, Rocky Mountain Research Station. 97 p.

Abstract

This annotated bibliography documents the research that has been conducted on the Great Basin Experimental Range (GBER, also known as the Utah Experiment Station, Great Basin Station, the Great Basin Branch Experiment Station, Great Basin Experimental Center, and other similar name variants) over the 102 years of its existence. Entries were drawn from the original abstracts or summaries when those were included in the original document. When no abstract or summary was provided the authors produced summaries for inclusion. One hundred and ninety-one works are included and indexed by date, type of publication, subject matter, and author. The works are divided into the following categories (some of which are interrelated): Community Ecology, Disturbance (Grazing) Ecology, Fire Ecology, Historical and Site Descriptions, Livestock Management, Mammal Ecology, Methodology, Plant Autoecology, Plant Physiology, Plant Taxonomy or Status, Range Ecology and Range Management, Research Needs Assessment, Revegetation and Restoration Ecology, Site Evaluation and Species Performance, Soil Biology and Ecology, and Watershed Ecology. One hundred and three authors are included among who are some eminent scientists that have made fundamental contributions to the body of natural resource science.

Keywords: Great Basin Experimental Range, Great Basin Experiment Station, Utah Experiment Station, Great Basin Station, livestock grazing, rangeland ecology, revegetation, species trials, watershed ecology

Authors

E. Durant McArthur, Emeritus Scientist, U.S. Department of Agriculture, Forest Service, Shrub Sciences Laboratory, Rocky Mountain Research Station.

Bryce A. Richardson, Research Geneticist, U.S. Department of Agriculture, Forest Service, Shrub Sciences Laboratory, Rocky Mountain Research Station, and Scientist-in-charge, Great Basin Experimental Range.

Stanley G. Kitchen, Research Botanist, U.S. Department of Agriculture, Forest Service, Shrub Sciences Laboratory, Rocky Mountain Research Station.

Great Basin Experimental Range: Annotated Bibliography[1]

E. Durant McArthur[2], Bryce A. Richardson[3] and Stanley G. Kitchen[4]

Introductory Note: Entries qualify for inclusion if they were conducted in whole or part at the Great Basin Experimental Range (GBER, also known as the Utah Experiment Station, Great Basin Station, the Great Basin Branch Experiment Station, Great Basin Experimental Center, and other similar name variants). They do not qualify merely by the author having worked at GBER when the research was performed or prepared. Entries were drawn from the original abstracts or summaries when those were included in the original document. The conclusions are those of the original authors. Likewise, (1) taxonomic treatments are those of the original authors with our occasional annotations for clarification and (2) tense is that of the original. However if the original was presented in first person point of view it was modified to third person point of view to provide internal homogeneity in the document.

The Great Basin Experimental Range names and function have changed with the times since the site was selected in 1911 and research and facility development started in 1912. Since 1997, Snow College has managed the headquarters area as the Great Basin Environmental Education Center (GBEEC). In its beginnings research at the GBER was not clearly separated from other Forest Service functions although research was clearly the primary purpose of the Great Basin Station as the facility was then known. The Station was one of the key elements that coalesced into the Intermountain Forest and Range Experiment Station (now part of the Rocky Mountain Research Station) when the network of nationwide geographical Forest Service Research Stations was established in 1930. Research was and is conducted within the Great Basin Experimental Range, which comprises some 4,600 acres in the Ephraim (Cottonwood Creek) Canyon watershed ranging from 6,700 to 10,500 feet in elevation. Research conducted from and overseen from the GBER, however, was not confined to the Great Basin Experimental Range per se,

---

[1] Entries qualify for inclusion if they were conducted in whole or part at the Great Basin Experimental Range, which has also been known as the Utah Experiment Station, the Great Basin Experiment Station, The Great Basin Branch Station, and the Great Basin Experimental Area or were based on GBER research in whole or part.

[2] Emeritus Scientist, U.S. Department of Agriculture, Forest Service, Shrub Sciences Laboratory, Rocky Mountain Research Station.

[3] Research Geneticist, U.S. Department of Agriculture, Forest Service, Shrub Sciences Laboratory, Rocky Mountain Research Station and Scientist-in-charge, Great Basin Experimental Range.

[4] Research Botanist, U.S. Department of Agriculture, Forest Service, Shrub Sciences Laboratory, Rocky Mountain Research Station.

but expanded out on other lands in the Manti National Forest (now Manti-La Sal National Forest) and beyond. The headquarters complex first buildings were started in 1912 and completed by 1914 with additions in the late 1920s and a new phase of building began with the help of Civilian Conservation Corps (CCC) labor in the 1930s. Other improvements were also built to facilitate the research studies of the Great Basin Station. These include gauging stations, water catchments basins, grazing exclosures and other fences, and the Alpine Cabin. Overs the course of time nearly 200 research publications have been produced in the areas of range management, watershed, vegetation composition and dynamics, plant adaptation, plant phenology, vigor, and nutrition; and silvicultural studies. The Experimental Range has also served a vital education and training function. Some of the eminent natural resource scientists who began their careers or established reputations here include Arthur Sampson, Fredrick Baker, W. R. Chapline, C. L. Forsling, Raymond Price, Lincoln Ellison, and A. Perry Plummer.

Acknowledgments: The authors are grateful for reviews of earlier versions of this manuscript by David Anderson, National Security Technologies; Liane Ellison Norman, poet and author; and Alison Whittaker, Utah Division of Wildlife Resources, Great Basin Research Center. Each reviewer has insight from experience gained from working or living at the GBER. The authors are also grateful to science librarians Mike Goates of Brigham Young University, Laura Bojanowski of the USDA Forest Service Rocky Mountain Research Station, and Laura Hutchinson of the USDA Forest Service Northern Research Station who were helpful in obtaining many of the documents included in this work.

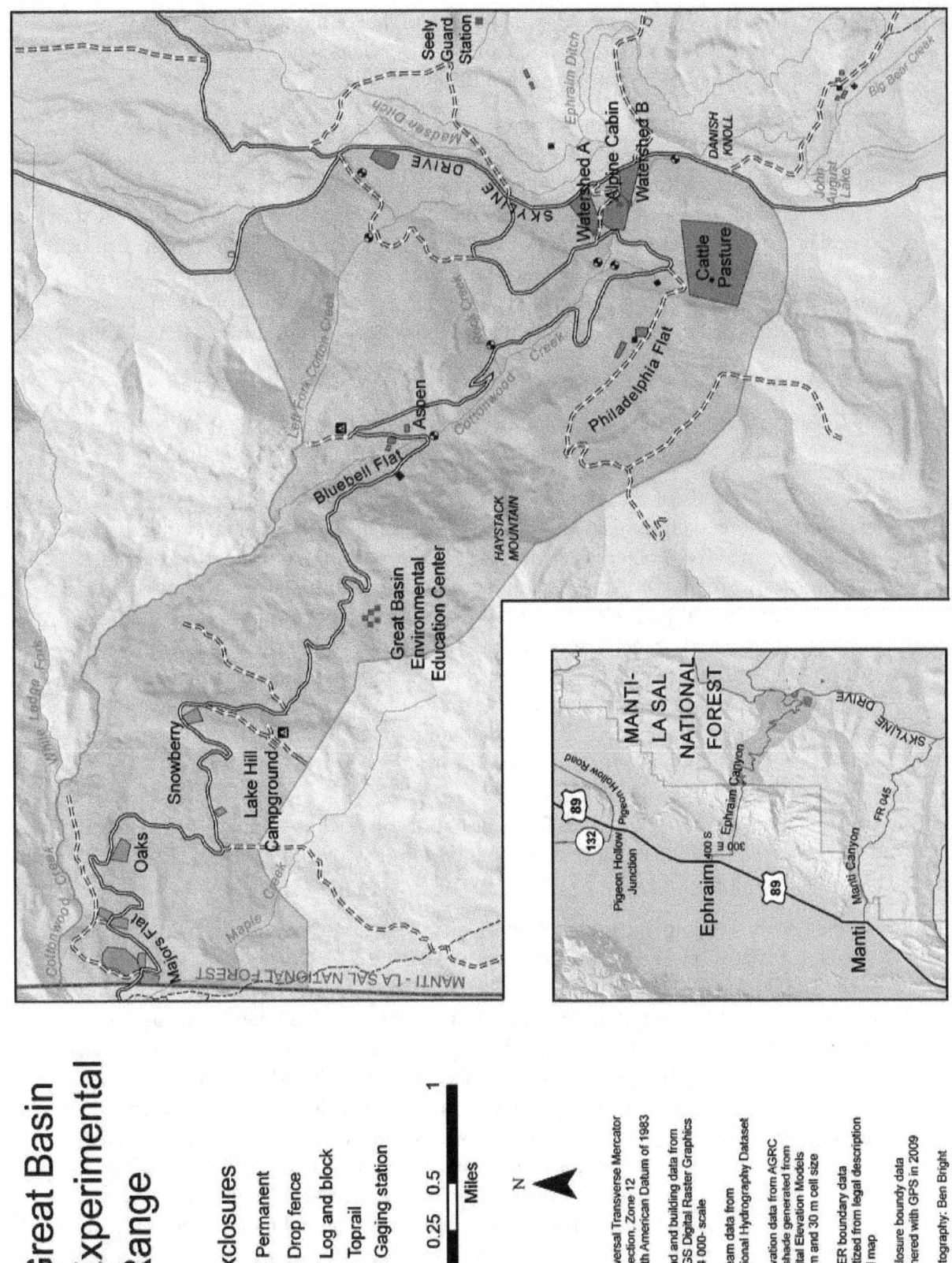

Great Basin Experimental Range

Exclosures
- Permanent
- Drop fence
- Log and block
- Toprail
- Gaging station

0 0.25 0.5 1 Miles

N

Universal Transverse Mercator projection, Zone 12 North American Datum of 1983

Road and building data from USGS Digital Raster Graphics 1:24 000-scale

Stream data from National Hydrography Dataset

Elevation data from AGRC Hillshade generated from Digital Elevation Models 10 m and 30 m cell size

GBER boundary data digitized from legal description and map

Exclosure boundy data gathered with GPS in 2009

Cartography: Ben Bright

001. Adams, Mary Beth; Loughry, Linda; Plaugher, Linda. 2004. Experimental Forests and Ranges of the USDA Forest Service. Gen. Tech. Rep. NE-321. Newton Square, PA: Northeastern Research Station. 178 p.

The Great Basin Experimental Range is among the inventory listed in this report. The USDA Forest Service has an outstanding scientific resource in the 77 Experimental Forests and Ranges that exist across the United States and its territories. These valuable scientific resources incorporate a broad range of climates, forest types, research emphases, and history. This publication describes each of the research sites within the Experimental Forest and Range network, providing information about history, climate, vegetation, soils, long-term data bases, research history and research products, as well as identifying collaborative opportunities, and providing contact information.

002. Alder, Guy Michael. 1970. Age-profiles of aspen forests in Utah and northern Arizona. Salt Lake City, UT: University of Utah. 31 p. Thesis.

A total of 44 stands of aspen were located on a variety of sites throughout Utah and into Arizona including a stand in the Great Basin Experimental Range. Ages for mature trees were obtained from cores taken with an increment borer. Stand age profiles were drawn using percent sum density within 5-year age class intervals. The traditional concept of even aged stands was not supported by the data. Instead, mature trees generally occurred in groups in which ages were somewhat normally distributed. Correlations between age and diameter, and diameter and height yielded highly significant, positive correlation coefficients. Inter- and intra-stand variation was considerably less than anticipated from such a wide-ranging set of age, diameter, and height measurements.

003. Aldous, C. M. 1951. The feeding habits of pocket gophers (*Thomomys talpoides moorei*) in the high mountain ranges of central Utah. Journal of Mammalogy 32(1): 84-87.

Studies of the feeding and storage habits of the pocket gopher were made on the Wasatch Plateau (Great Basin Experimental Range) in Utah at an elevation of 9000-10,000 feet. Work was conducted on fenced plots, which prevented grazing by livestock. While the animals are primarily of subterranean habits, it was found that they utilize considerable quantities of surface vegetation in the immediate vicinity of their mounds. A survey of clipped plants under 511 fresh mounds revealed that 48 species were involved in what amounted to almost complete removal of vegetation. Much of the plant cuttings was stored and used as food. However, some plants were cut and stored, which were not subsequently used for forage. It was suspected that the clear cutting of vegetation at prospective mound sites was partly a measure to facilitate subsequent mound formation. Among foods utilized in underground foraging, dandelion roots were most prominent. Tubers of *Stellaria* and bulbs of *Claytonia* ranked second and third, respectively. The relative amount of underground plant portions in storage was determined by excavating a runway at each of five different sites.

USDA Forest Service Gen. Tech. Rep. RMRS-GTR-305WWW. 2013

4

004. Antrei, Albert. 1982. Zion stands with hills surrounded (floods, conservation, and the Manti National Forest). Chapter 9. In: Antrei, Albert C. T.; Scow, Ruth T., eds. The other forty-niners, a topical history of Sanpete County, Utah 1849-1983. Salt Lake City, UT: Western Epics: 193-231.

This is a detailed chronicle of the conditions leading up to the establishment of the Manti Forest Reserve by President Theodore Roosevelt in 1903. The forest reserve with later organizational consolidations became part of the Manti National Forest and then the Manti-La Sal National Forest. Solution to the severe vegetative denudation and soil loss that brought on a citizens petition for watershed protection through the Forest Service also motivated the establishment of a research station in Ephraim Canyon of the Wasatch Plateau, Manti National Forest in 1912. The roles citizens like Lauritz Nielson of Ephraim and Mayor L. R. Anderson of Manti, National Forest System administrators like A. W. Jensen and J. W. Humphrey, and Great Basin Experimental Range scientists like Arthur W. Sampson, Lincoln Ellison, and A. Perry Plummer played in the conservation history and pioneering science discoveries are blended with Sanpete County community life by the author who himself was an employee of the Great Basin Experimental Range and later a school teacher and community leader in Sanpete County.

005. Antrei, Albert. 1993. To whom this may concern, landmarks of a liberal education. Manti, UT: The Universal Impression. 339 p.

This memoir includes colorful firsthand accounts of life at the Great Basin Experimental Station in the 1930s and 1940s with some forwarding through time as the author put down roots in the Sanpete Valley community. To wit: …I descended from that bus in Ephraim…on June Sunday (in 1936). As the bus departed I stood alone on the corner occupied by the D. W. Anderson Drug Company. I was as lost as that needle somebody dropped once in haystack, and I felt just as unlikely ever to be found again. …Down the street from me a lone sinner was breaking the Sabbath, heading for a stack of hay somewhere with a team of horses hitched up to an empty, chuckling hay wagon. Since it was a Sunday, the streets were otherwise properly empty, resembling a ghost town deserted the day before. I saw not a single automobile or tractor… I came to Utah to fill a job… My job was to help with the gathering of data in the field for research projects that were to be analyzed during the winter months in Ogden, Utah, at the Intermountain Forest and Range Experiment Station by scientists in range botany and soil erosion. All of the field work took place on summer range in Ephraim Canyon. Winter range research was conducted at the "Desert Station" about 50 miles west of Milford, Utah, and spring-fall range problems were studied at a station north of Dubois, Idaho. … Between June 1 and about October 1, I went to town with other station technicians to meet the girls. I was making about $125 per month, and every Saturday afternoon (we worked until noon) I went to town for a little R & R, to last until the station truck left for the station again usually about midnight. There was a movie theater in Ephraim and on Saturday nights an open-air dancing pavilion. I was not interested in church on Sunday, so on Sunday I remained at the foot of Haystack Mountain (Station Headquarters), either reminiscent or nurturing a headache. Religion did not bother me, and I did not bother it. I drank a little, which in Utah is the same as drinking a whole lot, and I smoked a pipe; moderately, I thought. But again here in Utah one curl of smoke means a forest fire...

006. Bailey, Reed W. 1945. Determining trend of range-watershed conditions to success in management. Journal of Forestry 43(10): 733-737.

Accurate determination of the condition and trend of the plant cover and soil mantle, site by site, is considered the key to satisfactory range-watershed management. Many unsatisfactory range-watershed situations are attributed largely to an inadequate understanding of conditions and trend, including a tendency to rely upon single-factor indices rather than to consider all of the observable site factors. As a solution, the author advocates further research in ecology and soils, a fuller use of range condition and trend in surveys and inspections, and higher professional qualifications for range-watershed managers. When factors entering into successes and failures in range management are considered, when the meaning of range condition and trend is analyzed, and when the uses to which knowledge of range condition and trend can be put are recognized; it becomes obvious that the accurate determination of condition and trend should rate high in the science and art of range management. The conclusion that the condition and trend of range-watershed lands are the basis on which policies are formulated and upon which action is taken is inescapable. Viewed in the light, condition and trend should have an important place in range inventories and should be the essential guides in laying out specific range-management plans. Certainly they constitute the heart of range inspection and the basis for considering programs. The observations and research that lead to this report were obtained, in part, from the Great Basin Experimental Range.

007. Bailey, Reed W. 1948. Forest and range research in Utah and the Intermountain Region. Utah Magazine 10(9): 6-7, 24-25.

Thirty-six years ago, forest and range research had its rather humble beginning in Utah. Four men drove up the winding Ephraim Canyon road in a wagon in June of 1912. The trip was exploratory; their purpose, to find a suitable spot for an experiment station at which research on erosion and related watershed matters could be conducted. The flood of 1909 had drawn attention to the canyon. The need for greater knowledge of flood causes from range watersheds, the suitability of the terrain, and the variety of plant life all made Ephraim Canyon a likely choice. This site ultimately became the Great Basin Experimental Range. Several lines of research are conducted by the Intermountain Station; there are six broad types performed by the station scientists. These are (1) watershed management and protection studies, which seek out ways of obtaining maximum utilization of the forage and range resources without inducing soil erosion or flood runoffs; (2) grazing management studies aimed at determining the grazing capacity and proper seasonal use of the various types of range so as to support the greatest number of livestock and wildlife year after year; (3) range reseeding investigations designed to determine what types of native or introduced grasses and shrubs are most suited to rangelands and how they can be planted and maintained; (4) range economics research to relate the findings of range research to social and economic conditions; (5) forest management studies concerned at present principally with harvesting and restocking of ponderosa pine areas; and (6) flood control surveys that develop programs of land use and treatment for erosion and flood control.

008. Bailey, Reed W.; Connaughton, Charles A. 1936. Watershed protection. In: The western range, 74th U.S. Congress, 2nd Session. Washington, DC: Senate Document 199: 303-339.

This broad review of watershed conditions includes a section on the Great Basin Experimental Range. The role of vegetation (in the conservation of watershed resource) had to be ascertained quantitatively by detailed investigation. The first of these investigations of any consequence on western rangeland was instituted by the Forest Service on the Great Basin Experimental Range on the Wasatch Plateau near Ephraim, Utah, in 1912, where a study was made of the runoff and erosion from two grazing areas of about 10 acres each, fairly similar except for the cover of vegetation. Area A had an original plant density of 16 percent and Area B a density of 40 percent. Both areas were grazed and for the 6 years, 1915 to 1920, the cover was maintained at the original densities. During the period 1921 to 1923 Area A was allowed to revegetate until its density approximately equaled that of Area B. From 1924 to 1929 both areas were grazed and maintained at equal densities. With Area A in a depleted condition, the runoff percent and sediment removed were approximately 4.1 and 5.4 times greater than Area B. As the plant cover was gradually restored on the former, these differences diminished until the ratios for runoff percent and sediment were only 2.9 and 2.8. Finally, when the densities of the plant cover were made comparable, the runoff percent from the two areas was practically the same, and the excess of silt removed from A was reduced from 109.1 to 11.5 cubic feet. This reduction of silt removed from Area A following revegetation has a far greater significance than merely the reduction of soil movement, because of its indirect effect on the future rate of absorption and percolation of the soil.

009. Baker, Fredrick S. 1918. Aspen as a temporary forest type. Journal of Forestry 16(3): 294-303.

It must be admitted at the outset that the aspen stands of the Great Basin are certainly not ephemeral, but have probably existed much as they are now for many generations and will doubtless last for many more. Accordingly, they have the appearance of permanence. In Colorado and New Mexico, where conditions are similar, the temporary nature of the aspen stands is not questioned, because the coniferous climax is generally further advanced and there is not an appearance of stability or long duration. Duration, however, is no criterion of true stability. As defined by the Forest Service, a permanent or climax type is "a forest type which will eventually take possession of and perpetuate itself on any given area if natural conditions are undisturbed. Therefore if aspen is giving way to conifers at all within its "permanent" range, it is essentially transitory and a subclimax stage in succession. Observations and research that led to this publication came, in part, from the Great Basin Experimental Range.

010. Baker, Fredrick S. 1918. Aspen reproduction in relation to management. Journal of Forestry 16(4): 389-398.

Reproduction by root suckers is practically the only means by which aspen stands are regenerated in the Intermountain area. As conditions of climate and other factors that would influence reproduction are practically the same now as they have been for the last few centuries, it seems improbable that seed reproduction has been active for a very long time. That vegetative reproduction should still remain so vigorous is remarkable, when the usual rapid deterioration of coppice of other species is considered. It seems improbable, therefore, that any immediate deterioration in vigor of reproduction is to be expected. The management of aspen, therefore, becomes very simple. Since practically all the reproduction is by sprouts, the silvicultural system is obviously clear-cutting, since this gives rise to the maximum number of sprouts. Observations and research that led to this publication came, in part, from the Great Basin Experimental Range.

011. Baker, Fredrick S. 1921. Two races of aspen. Journal of Forestry 19(4): 412-413.

In the mountain ranges running north and south through the State of Utah, aspen (*Populus tremuloides*) is an exceptionally common tree at middle elevations, covering large areas with solid bodies of pure type, particularly in the Wasatch Mountains and the Wasatch and Fishlake Plateaus. In the spring when the leaves are unfolding it is commonly noted that the leafing time of adjacent bodies is quite dissimilar. Not infrequently a line can be traced for upwards of a mile through the aspen where on the one side, the leaves are half developed and on the other the buds are just bursting. This line is almost invariably clear cut and distinct with little intermingling of the two forms. The boundary is apparently not determined by topography or soil conditions, as it may run up and down slopes or across them, or perhaps more frequently it will pursue a serpentine course entirely independent of topography. While spring leafing is the most striking feature in which these two forms of aspen differ, there are also other characteristics which are apparent. The leaves on the trees that come out first last longest in the fall, as a rule, although there is less consistency in this matter than spring development, due apparently to the uneven action of frosts in the mountainous country. Furthermore, the trees that leaf out earlier have neighboring clones that are characterized by a somewhat yellowish or brownish tinged bark when compared to those that leaf out later. Measurements in a 44-year-old stand on the grounds of the Great Basin Experiment Station (Great Basin Experimental Range) show a difference of only 0.03 inch in the diameter of the "white" and "yellow" trees, however, in favor of the "white," while the finest stand in the region around the Great Basin Experiment Station is "yellow" near the upper limits of aspen in an Engelmann spruce burn.

012. Baker, Frederick S. 1925. Aspen in the central Rocky Mountain region. Tech. Bull. 1291. Washington, DC: U.S. Department of Agriculture. 47 p.

USDA Forest Service Gen. Tech. Rep. RMRS-GTR-305WWW. 2013

8

The detailed results reported in this bulletin were carried out chiefly on the Ephraim Canyon watershed of the Manti National Forest, in central Utah (the Great Basin Experimental Range). The results, however, in a very general way, cover the aspen in the entire central Rocky Mountain region, including Wyoming, Colorado, Utah, Nevada, southern Idaho, and a little of northern Arizona and New Mexico. The report gives distribution information and describes the tree and its plant community including leaf, flower, seed, bark and leaf characteristics; growth forms; climatic and soil and moisture requirements; quality growth sites; susceptibility to the injurious factors including fungi, insects, mammals, and abiotic factors; reproduction of conifers associated with aspen; associated species; growth characteristics including height, diameter, yield, and volume; thinning; wood properties; uses; management; silvicultural systems; and succession.

013. Baker, Frederick S. 1925. Character of the soil in relation to the reproduction of western yellow pine. Journal of Forestry 23(7-8): 630-634.

The opinion is very frequently expressed by foresters throughout the West that western yellow pine reproduces best in sandy soil. In some places where growing conditions are first class, reproduction may be found upon heavy, clayey soils it is true, but in general it has been noted that where conditions are rather difficult for reproduction, a sandy soil is evidently much superior to a heavy clay soil. No investigations have yet shown exactly why this is so, or indeed whether it is actually a fact connected with the soil at all. There is a constantly increasing mass of information, however, regarding the factors that influence the reproduction of western yellow pine and in order to add a little evidence to this body of information, the results of an experiment carried out some years ago at the Great Basin Experiment Station (Great Basin Experimental Range) in Utah, are presented. Data show that the development of western yellow pine is conditioned more by the physical character of the soil under consideration than any other factor in usual forest soils, and that acidity is not a limiting factor. Of course, when alkalinity, or possibly acidity, rises to extreme points these factors may have considerable bearing on the growth of seedlings. While lightness of soil tends to favor the establishment of the young seedlings, their subsequent growth, except on very heavy clays and other unfavorable soils, seems to be determined by the degree of fertility (organic content) of the soil.

014. Baker, F. S.; Korstian, C. F. 1931. Suitability of brush lands in the Intermountain region for the growth of natural or planted western yellow pine forests. Tech. Bull. No. 256. Washington, DC: U.S. Department of Agriculture. 83 p.

Western yellow pine, which is otherwise rather generally distributed throughout the western United States, is absent in a belt extending from the Gulf of California northeastward into west-central Montana. In northern Utah and southeastern Idaho, where this belt is several hundred miles wide, the elevations at which the pine is commonly found in other parts of the West are occupied by brush-land shrubs. A comparison of this brush-land belt with the natural pine zone reveals both similarities and differences in climatic and soil conditions. It is among the differences in these conditions that the factors that make the brush lands unsuitable for the germination and early development of the yellow pine seedlings are to be found. A comparison of conditions in the western yellow pine zones to the north and south with those of the intervening brush lands shows that no significant differences in temperature exist and no notable differences in total annual precipitation but the distribution of rainfall during the summer months in the brush lands is notably different from that either to the north or south. Observations and research that led to this publication came, in part, from the Great Basin Experimental Range.

015. Baker, F. S.; Korstian, C. F.; Fetherolf, N. J. 1921. Snowshoe rabbits and conifers in the Wasatch Mountains of Utah. Ecology 2(4): 304-310.

Snowshoe rabbits are present in large numbers throughout the Wasatch Mountains. Their food during the winter months consists principally of the buds and tender twigs of conifers, and they are therefore a serious menace to natural reproduction as well as to plantations. In localities where rabbits are numerous, injury from this cause materially reduces height-growth of coniferous seedlings and saplings. With the destruction of a large number of coyotes, the principal natural enemy of rabbits, there has been a considerable increase in the number of rabbits and a corresponding increase in the damage to conifers. Poisoning is the most feasible method of rabbit control on large areas. Fencing is necessary where absolute protection is desired on small areas. Formulae are given for preparing poison bait. Observations and research that led to this publication came, in part, from the Great Basin Experimental Range.

016. Barnes, Burton V. 1975. Phenotypic variation of trembling aspen in Western North America. Forest Science 21(3): 319-328.

Phenotypic variation of leaf, bud, and twig characters was investigated in 1,257 trembling aspen clones at 206 locations in 7 states and 1 Canadian province. Early leaves from seasonally determinate shoots of the lower crown were sampled to minimize intraclonal variation. Univariate and multivariate analyses revealed a clinal south-north gradient in leaf shape, size, and tooth number from southern Utah to northern Montana and Idaho. Nearly all clones had pubescent buds and shoots; these characteristics were most pronounced in Vancouver Island populations. Leaves from the Colorado and Columbia Plateaus closely resembled leaves of fossil Miocene and Pliocene aspen. Clones from mostly unglaciated areas were larger than those from the northern part of the study area. Observations and research that led to this publication came, in part, from the Great Basin Experimental Range.

017. Baskin, Carol C.; Meyer, Susan E.; Baskin, Jerry M. 1995. Two types of morphophysiological dormancy in seeds of two genera (*Osmorhiza* and *Erythronium*) with an Arcto-Tertiary distribution pattern. American Journal of Botany 82(3): 293-298.

Temperature requirements for embryo growth and germination were determined for seeds of *Osmorhiza occidentalis, O. chilensis,* and *Erythronium gladiflorum* collected in western North America (Utah). Initially, embryos were 1.2, 0.6, and 0.8 mm in length, respectively, and they grew to 9.4, 9.2, and 4.1 mm, respectively, before germination occurred. Embryo growth and germination occurred during cold stratification (1, 5, 5/1 °C), without a warm stratification pretreatment. However, warm stratification pretreatments at 30/15 °C increased rates of embryo growth in *O. occidentalis* and *E. grandiflorum* seeds subsequently moved to low temperatures, and germination rates in all three species. Optimum germination temperatures were 1,5, or 5/1 °C; gibberellic acid did not substitute for cold stratification. Thus, seeds of the three species have deep complex morphophysiological dormancy (MPD). Two species each of *Osmorhiza* and *Erythronium* from eastern North America have a nondeep complex MPD and require warming followed by cold stratification for germination. The disjunct species in these genera with an Arcto-Tertiary distribution pattern can have different types of MPD. It is suggested that deep complex MPD may have been derived from nondeep complex MPD. Observations and research that led to this publication came, in part, from the Great Basin Experimental Range.

018. Blauer, A. Clyde; McArthur, E. Durant; Stevens, Richard; Nelson, Sheldon D. 1993. Evaluation of roadside stabilization and beautification plantings in south-central Utah. Res. Pap. INT-462. Ogden, UT: U.S. Department of Agriculture, Forest Service, Intermountain Research Station. 65 p.

Numerous roadside plantings at semiarid sites in the south-central Utah counties of Juab, Sanpete, and Sevier were intended to stabilize roadsides with plants harmonizing with the natural vegetation. The plantings, originally for demonstration, began in the 1950s. They included bareroot transplants and direct seedings. Soils and geologic substrates at six sites were analyzed for 15 characteristics. Plant performance and survival was summarized for 27 sites. Thirty species established well by direct seeding and 62 species established well from transplants. Numerous other species have also persisted at the planting sites but are not as vigorous or as well adapted. Direct seedings were principally grasses and forbs; the transplants were mainly shrubs. Thirty-six species showed enough recruitment to sustain themselves on the sites. Observations and research that led to this publication came, in part, from the Great Basin Experimental Range.

019. Blauer, A. Clyde; Plummer, A. Perry; McArthur, E. Durant; Stevens, Richard; Giunta, Bruce C. 1975. Characteristics and hybridization of important Intermountain shrubs. I. Rose family. Res. Pap. INT-169. Ogden, UT: U.S. Department of Agriculture, Forest Service, Intermountain Forest and Range Experiment Station. 35 p.

This paper reviews the state of knowledge, records observations, and presents original data for important Intermountain rosaceous shrubs. A key is given to aid recognition of taxa. Each species treated is described and it hybridization, distribution and habitat, and use are reviewed. Pioneer hybridization studies conducted in part on the Great Basin Experimental Range, on the compatible genera *Cowania* (cliffrose), *Fallugia* (Apache plume), and *Purshia* (bitterbrush) are presented.

020. Bleak, A. T. 1959. Germinative characteristics of grass seed under snow. Journal of Range Management 12(6): 298-302.

Moistened seeds of smooth brome, Tualatin oatgrass and tall oatgrass and pregerminated seeds of smooth brome developed visible radicles or shoots in thawed soil under a deep snow cover. Seeds in small cloth bags placed under one-half inch of soil and permanent winter snow cover on November 30, 1956, and January 4, 1957, were removed at monthly intervals. Snow depth varied from 14 inches in November to 90 inches in April. By May 13, when the snow cover was still 46 inches deep, some seeds of smooth brome and tall oatgrass had developed primary roots over 1½ inches long and shoots were just emerging from the soil surface. Viability of pre-germinated seeds of smooth brome and Tualatin oatgrass decreased substantially more than seeds of the comparable control lots. Percent decrease in viability under the deep snow cover was greatest in the old seed of Tualatin oatgrass with low initial viability. Additional observations on conditions at or near the soil surface were made in pits dug in the deep snow to plant and remove seed. Frozen soil present in the fall and early winter began thawing in February. In March, April, and May the soil at a depth of one-half inch was moist and frost-free. Decomposition of cotton bags, fine leaves and stems, and other organic material by fungi and other organisms was rather rapid in the moist, frost-free soil under deep snow. Growth of established perennial grasses under the snow cover was observed in the pit dug in March and in all pits dug later. Observations and research that led to this publication came, in part, from the Great Basin Experimental Range.

021. Bleak, A. T. 1968. Growth and yield of legumes in mixtures with grasses on a mountain range. Journal of Range Management 21(4): 259-261.

Nine legumes, including three strains of variegated alfalfa, were planted in mixture with each of four grasses in the fall of 1950. Alfalfa A-169 was the most productive legume. In 1965 it yielded 100 lb/acre, about 35percent more than cicer milkvetch or Ladak alfalfa and 160 lb/acre more than sickle milkvetch or Rhizoma alfalfa. Siberian alfalfa was clearly inferior to all the above. Flat pea, birdsfoot trefoil, and perennial vetch disappeared from the plots early in the study. Intermediate and crested wheatgrasses were more productive than smooth brome, both in combination with legumes and as pure stands. The highest yielding plots in 1965 were those originally sown to mountain brome. This short-lived grass afforded less competition to the legumes that became well established prior to invasion by crested and intermediate wheatgrass or smooth brome grass. The use of a legume with grass, on the average, increased production by 144 lb/acre. Observations and research that led to this publication came, in part, from the Great Basin Experimental Range.

USDA Forest Service Gen. Tech. Rep. RMRS-GTR-305WWW. 2013

12

022. Bleak, Alvin T. 1970. Disappearance of plant material under a winter snow cover. Ecology 51(5): 915-917.

Disappearance of plant material from fine-mesh nylon bags occurred during the late fall, winter, or early spring when mountain ranges in central Utah are generally snow covered. Quantitative loss of matter from leaves and stems of two grasses and two broad-leaved forbs was mostly attributed to decomposition by fungi and bacteria and to leaching. Loss of material from bags in direct contact with the snow cover during two consecutive winter periods averaged 30 percent for the relatively coarse *Agropyron trachycaulum*, 39 percent for *Bromus inermis*, 48 percent for *Lupinus alpestris*, and 51 percent for *Mertensia arizonica* var, *leonardi*. The ratio of leaf to stem weights decreased with all aspects. Observations and research that led to this publication came, in part, from the Great Basin Experimental Range.

023. Bleak, A. T.; Plummer, A. Perry. 1954. Grazing crested wheatgrass by sheep. Journal of Range Management 7(2): 63-68.

Planting depleted spring-fall range with adapted grasses in the Intermountain region is now an important enterprise. Crested wheatgrass (*Agropyron cristatum*) is presently the best for seeding these ranges and is in widespread use. A grazing study with sheep was conducted on six, 1½-acre dryland pastures in typical spring-fall range in Utah with crested wheatgrass as the dominant species. Beardless bluebunch wheatgrass and bulbous bluegrass occurred as secondary components. Three intensities of use were applied (light, moderate and heavy) with grazing starting when crested wheatgrass was 2 to 3 inches high (early) and 4 to 5 inches high (deferred). After 7 years of grazing, injurious effects were obvious where crested wheatgrass had been heavily utilized (88 percent use). Under heavy grazing, production decreased, most grass clumps were dead in the middle, plants were small, and there was a marked growth of Russian thistle generally over the pastures. Although production declined with aging of the seeded stands, crested wheatgrass appears to have maintained equally good production under light (59 percent) and moderate (71 percent) use during this first 7 years. Observations and research that led to this publication came, in part, from the Great Basin Experimental Range.

024. Brown, Peter M.; Heyerdahl, Emily K.; Kitchen, Stanley G.; Weber, Marc H. 2008. Climate effects on historical fires (1630-1900) in Utah. International Journal of Wildland Fire 17(1): 28-39.

The association between climate effects and fire occurrence from 1630 to 1900 were constructed for a new set of cross dated fire-scar chronologies from 18 forested sites in Utah, including the Great Basin Experimental Range, and one site in eastern Nevada. Years with regionally synchronous fires (31 years with fire at ≥20 percent of sites) occurred during drier than average summers and years with no fires at any site (100 years) were wetter than average. Antecedent wet summers were associated with regional-fire years in mixed-conifer and ponderosa pine forest types, possibly by affecting fine fuel amount and continuity. NINO3 (an index of the El Niño-Southern Oscillation, ENSO) was significantly low during regional-fire years (La Niñas) and significantly high during non-fire years (El Niños). NINO3 also was high during years before regional-fire years. Although regional fire years occurred nearly twice as often as expected when NINO3 and the Pacific Decadal Oscillation were both in their cool (negative) phases, this pattern was not statistically significant. Palmer drought Severity Index was important for fire occurrence in ponderosa pine and mixed-conifer forests across the study area but ENSO forcing was seen only in southeastern sites. Results support findings from previous fire and climate studies, including a possible geographic pivot point in Pacific basin teleconnections at ~ 40 °N.

025. Chapline, W. R. 1929. Range research of the U.S. Forest Service. Journal of American Society of Agronomy 21(6): 644-649.

The continued prosperity of the range livestock industry depends on improving and maintaining the range resource. This industry, with ranches and livestock worth nearly 2 billion dollars, makes use of 587 million acres of rangelands or nearly one-third of the total land area of the United States. Nearly 70 percent of the feed for all the livestock in the 11 far western states is obtained from grazing the native forage on timbered and other rangeland. The productivity of national forest ranges has increased about 25 percent in the last 15 to 20 years through regulation and the application of improved principles developed by research. On the other hand, most other range areas have continued to decline until, on the average, they are at least 50 percent below their producing possibilities. The range research of the Forest Service is largely concentrated at three stations: the Great Basin Experimental Range in central Utah, the Santa Rita Range Reserve in southern Arizona, and the Jornada Range Reserve in southern New Mexico.

026. Chapline, W. R. 1931. Erosion dares the West. American Forests 37(8): 470-474.

On an experimental watershed on the Wasatch Plateau in Utah (Great Basin Experimental Range) where past overgrazing had depleted the vegetative cover until it occupied only about 16 percent of the surface, an average of 8 to 9 tons per acre of soil were eroded annually between 1915 and 1920. Starting with the latter date, effort was made to increase the plant cover as rapidly as possible by artificial and natural reseeding and since 1923 the watershed has supported an average cover of 40 percent. By comparing results with a check watershed, it was found that the increase in vegetation from a 16 percent cover to one of 40 percent brought about a 64 percent reduction in surface run-off from summer rains and a 54 percent reduction in sediment removed by these rain storms. These Utah studies by the Intermountain Station show that under extreme depletion of soil and plant cover it requires many years of careful management to restore watershed values. They also show that total exclusion of livestock from ranges is not necessary except where the plant cover has been almost eliminated and the fertile parts of the soil carried away. They emphasize the essential need for effective regulation of grazing.

USDA Forest Service Gen. Tech. Rep. RMRS-GTR-305WWW. 2013

14

027. Chapline, W. R. 1944. The history of western range research. Agricultural History 18(3): 127-143.

Range research furnishes basic information, guides, and procedures for the intelligent use and management of range lands for grazing. The growth of this field of science in relation to the western range has been gradual, following the development of the West and reflecting the increasing realization of the need for more and still more facts to obtain the highest use and maximum benefits of the Nation's vast resources. The collection of information on western grazing started with the notes and observations made by early explorers, military leaders, and missionaries. Range research progressed very slowly during the opening and settling of the western grazing grounds by the cattle kings and homesteaders. Its real growth began in response to the necessities arising from the Federal policy of forest reservation and administration; administration of the forest reserves made regulated use of the range just as necessary as regulated utilization of the timber. The building up of a sound body of data for stock ranges at grazing capacity during suitable seasons, and development of range research has lagged far behind the need. Deterioration of ranges still exists in large areas. Although some formal grazing experiments were begun by 1910, the development of range research has approached the needed comprehensive program only since about 1935. This development has been the result of recognition of the value and need for range research accompanied by intensified use of public and private ranges in a progressive national agriculture enterprise. Observations and research that led to this publication came, in part, from the Great Basin Experimental Range.

028. Clark, Ira. 1945. Variability in growth characteristics of forage plants on summer range in central Utah. Journal of Forestry 43(4): 273-283.

Marked variability in the growth characteristics of range grasses was demonstrated in a four-year study of several grasses common on mountainous summer ranges in the Intermountain region. A lack of constancy in growth form was the rule rather than the exception. This is due to seasonal weather conditions, density of stand, previous grazing treatment, available moisture and mineral nutrients, and other site factors. Variability in yield and growth characteristics in range plants from year to year and from site to site is of practical significance to stockmen and range managers since it greatly affects the accuracy and suitability of the various methods available for determining the current degree of range use. Observations and research that led to this publication came, in part, from the Great Basin Experimental Range.

029. Clary, Warren P.; Tiedemann, Arthur R. 1987. Distribution of biomass within small tree and shrub form *Quercus gambelii* stands. Forest Science 32(1): 234-242.

Gambel oak (*Quercus gambelii* Nutt.) occupies approximately 3.5 million ha in the states of Arizona, Colorado, New Mexico, and Utah. It is becoming recognized as an important fuelwood resource. Design of appropriate management strategies requires information on the biomass distribution characteristics within these stands. Biomass components of eight Gambel oak small tree and shrub form stands (clones) were sampled in Utah. Stem densities ranged from 5,000 to 34,000 per ha of clone. Mean stem diameters varied from 36 to 117 mm. Live stems averaged 4,992 g including dead branches, while standing dead stems averaged 1.347 g. Live biomass per occupied hectare averaged 124,388 kg including 40,704 kg of bole. The ratio of aboveground to belowground live biomasses was unusually low—44:56. Total aboveground and belowground biomass including detritus was 184,292 kg per hectare of clone. Observations and research that led to this publication came, in part, from the Great Basin Experimental Range.

030. Clary, Warren P.; Tiedemann, Arthur R. 1993. Bole volume growth in stems of *Quercus gambelii*. Great Basin Naturalist 53(2): 162-167.

Shrub-form and tree-form Gambel oak (*Quercus gambelii*) stands contain a potentially significant fuelwood resource. Information on their growth characteristics can form a basis for future stand management. Stem analyses showed that height growth of shrub-form stems essentially ceased after age 50, while tree-form stems continued to increase in height until approximately age 100. Both stem forms continued to increase in basal area and volume at a relatively constant rate as the stems increased in age and size. Increases in all size measures were substantially greater in tree-form stems than in shrub-form stems. Mean bole volume for tree-form stems at age 100 was over 16 times that of shrub-form stems. Sprouts from tree-form stands would reach minimum size for fuelwood marketing in approximately 45 years. Observations and research that led to this publication came, in part, from the Great Basin Experimental Range.

031. Costello, David F.; Price, Raymond. 1939. Weather and plant-development data as determinants of grazing periods on mountain range. Tech. Bull. No. 686. Washington, DC: U.S. Department of Agriculture. 31 p.

To determine proper opening grazing periods of mountain ranges it is important to have knowledge about (1) the normal growth and development of the principal forage plants at different altitudinal zones, (2) the fluctuation in seasonal growth and development of the plants from year to year, and (3) the more readily measured climatic factors related to the growth and development of the plants. Observations and measurements of weather and range plant development in Ephraim Canyon, Utah, by the Great Basin Branch (Great Basin Experimental Range) of the Intermountain Forest and Range Experiment Station during the 10-year period 1925-1934 furnish information on these problems. The vegetation in Ephraim Canyon with the elevational limits of the study is of three major types or zones: oakbrush, 6,500 to 8,000 feet; aspen-fir, 7,500 to 9,000 feet; and the spruce-fir, 9,000 feet and above. Temperature and precipitation vary between zones. Average monthly temperatures is 42.6, 30.0, and 32.5 °F. in the lower, middle, and upper zones respectively. Average annual precipitation for the same zones is 17.51, 29.48 and 20.01 inches. The average length of the growing season for different elevations

USDA Forest Service Gen. Tech. Rep. RMRS-GTR-305WWW. 2013

16

in Ephraim Canyon is 175 days at 7,000 feet; 160 days at 8,000 feet; 145 days at 9,000 feet; and 125 days at 10,000 feet. It is notable that each individual species of mountain range forage plant has its own specific rate of growth and development. Growth rates vary both within and between vegetation classes and each has a specific rate of development. Finally, earlier growth stages develop more rapidly than later stages. The rate of development varies with altitude, being delayed from 10 to 14 days for each 1,000-foot increase in elevation. Height growth at any particular date decreases with increase in elevation largely due to higher average temperatures at the lower altitudes.

032. Craddock, George W. 1948. Insuring Utah's water supplies through watershed research. Utah Magazine 10(9): 14-15, 27, 29.

Water supply issues of too little usable water and too much muddy water call for more knowledge about the runoff behavior of the mountainous watershed lands. Many questions need to be addressed. How do these watersheds yield their water? Has man, through his exploitation of the mineral forage and timber resources, increased the floods and the sediment load of the stream? If so, can eroding soil be stabilized and can erratic stream flow be brought under control? Additional questions include: Does timber harvesting, grazing, and construction damage watersheds to the extent that the resources on mountain watersheds need to be excluded from human use? Two laboratories in Utah have been developed to get answers to these important questions. The first of these was established in 1912 on the high plateau above Ephraim on the Wasatch Plateau known as the Great Basin Research Center (Great Basin Experimental Range). In 1933, a second laboratory—the Wasatch Research Center—was developed on the steep western front of the Wasatch Mountains east of Farmington. These are outdoor laboratories in which small and large watersheds are studied through the entire hydrologic cycle.

033. Craddock, George W. 1954. Water yield from snow as affected by consumptive water losses. In: Stockwell, Homer J.; Lamoreux, Wallace W.; Odell, John M.; Wilson, Milton T., publication committee. Proceedings of the Western Snow Conference, twenty-second annual meeting; 1954 April 19-21; Salt Lake City, UT. Fort Collins, CO: Colorado A and M College, Multigraph Service Bureau: 70-73.

The snow that accumulates each winter on high elevation forest and rangelands has long been known to be the principal source of the water supply for most of the West. The conservation of that snow resource has become a major concern as demands for more water have grown apace with the needs of an expanding economy. There are several possibilities of meeting the future water needs of the West. One is to build more storage dams and transmountain diversions. Another option is to tap more of the ground water basins. There is also room for reducing the waste of already developed water supplies by improving water conveyance systems and by using water more efficiently. In addition, there is the possibility of reducing the consumptive losses of snow water by altering the vegetation on the watershed lands where runoff begins. The idea of reducing evapo-transpiration losses of snow water by watershed management practices is both intriguing and hydrologically sound. There is evidence, however, that the benefits that may accrue from changing the plant cover may be offset by a number of adverse effects. The purpose of this paper is to point out some of these conflicting possibilities in the hope of clarifying the thinking about watershed management problems, especially those within the Intermountain region. Data from four kinds of summer range cover was collected at the Great Basin Research Center (Great Basin Experimental Range) in central Utah. The four kinds of cover included pure stands of smooth bromegrass, timothy, Kentucky bluegrass, and a mixture of dandelion and sweetsage. The latter mixture is commonly found on depleted, high elevation, herbaceous rangeland. The difference between the field moisture capacity of the soil following the spring snowmelt and the depleted moisture content in the fall plus the amount of summer rainfall provided a basis for estimating the seasonal evapotranspiration losses. The difference between the late fall soil moisture content and field capacity also provided a basis for determining differences in water recharge requirements and amounts of water that would be available for streamflow from the next year's snow pack. Estimates of forage production were obtained by clipping and weighing current plant growth. Smooth brome plots consumed the most water, produced the most forage, and made the most efficient use of the water consumed. The 350 pounds of forage per acre produced per inch of water consumed is about as good as can be obtained on irrigated valley lands. By comparison, areas with timothy consumed 0.79 inch less water and produced less than half as much forage. Kentucky bluegrass areas consumed about 1.00 inch less water than those with timothy but were more efficient in the use of water. The weed areas consumed the least water but were also by far the least efficient in forage production. The variability in the water consuming efficiency of these four types of summer range cover suggests the possibility of achieving different objectives on range watershed lands.

034. Croft, A. R. 1944. Evaporation from snow. Bulletin of the American Meteorological Society 25: 334-337.

A phase of the hydrologic cycle of drainage basins in the Intermountain Region about which more should be known is the loss of water by evaporation directly from the snow mantle. Snow that supplies most of the water for stream flow covers large parts of drainages from 4 to 8 months of each year; no doubt considerable water is lost by evaporation. A preliminary study was made of evaporation from snow under three site conditions on an important watershed of the Great Basin Experimental Range on the Wasatch Plateau in central Utah. A knowledge of water lost to evaporation from snow aids in obtaining a more complete understanding of the hydrologic cycle. In this region irrigation water is of extremely high economic value and much of that comes from melted snow. Timber stands make up a substantial part of the vegetation of the watershed; it may be possible through cutting methods to control wind movement so as to decrease evaporation and increase stream flow.

USDA Forest Service Gen. Tech. Rep. RMRS-GTR-305WWW. 2013

18

035. Croft, A. R. 1944. Snow melting and evaporation. Science 100(2591): 169-170.

Melting and evaporation of snow during the winter and spring seasons on the high mountains and plateaus of the Intermountain Region are processes of considerable interest to water users in the adjacent arid valleys because they have a direct bearing on the timeliness, rate and amount of stream flow that becomes available during the remainder of the year for irrigation, power, and other purposes. Records show that snow accumulates on the watershed lands during November 1 to April 1 to depths of from 4 to 10 feet, and that the snow mantle just prior to active melting in the spring may contain from 10 to 50 inches of water. Relatively little is known, about the rate at which the snow melts or the amount of water that is lost from the snow mantle by evaporation. To augment the meager knowledge of these phenomena, preliminary studies of snow melting and evaporation were conducted at elevations from 8,700 to 10,000 feet on a portion of the Wasatch Plateau in central Utah (Great Basin Experimental Range) during the snow melting season of 1942.

036. Croft, A. R.; Marston, Richard B. 1944. Some recharge-phenomena of a Wasatch Plateau watershed. Transactions, American Geophysical Union 1943: 460-464.

One of the biggest gaps in the knowledge of the hydrology of high watersheds of the Intermountain Region is the lack of understanding of the phenomena that occur from the time a deposit of snow begins to melt and the time that part of the melted snow-water appears as stream-flow. The part played by snow in watershed-recharge, snow-melting rates, and the factors that influence them—movement of melted-snow water through the snow, overland flow beneath snow and on bare soil-surfaces, infiltration-capacities of snow-covered surface and subsurface-soils, and duration and movement of gravitational water in the watershed-mantle—are some of the processes about which only meager knowledge, or none at all is available. This paper reports the results of measurements and observations of some of these phenomena on a 99-acre watershed inside the Manti Forest, on the west face of the Wasatch Plateau in central Utah on the Great Basin Experimental Range. This watershed is known as "A-B Drainage" and is one of the ten watersheds that range from 9 to 1,645 acres in area and are tributary to Ephraim Creek. The Intermountain Forest and Range Experiment Station is making comprehensive studies on the watersheds to determine the effect on stream-flow characteristics of mechanical water-flow-control structures located in the recharge-zone. The watersheds are now being calibrated for stream-flow. The data presented in this report are representative of those that are being secured during the calibration period.

037. Davis, James N. 2004. Research background. In: Monsen, Stephen B.; Stevens, Richard; Shaw, Nancy L., comps. Restoring western ranges and wildlands. Gen. Tech. Rep. RMRS GTR-136. Fort Collins, CO: U.S. Department of Agriculture, Forest Service, Rocky Mountain Research Station: 15-17.

Establishment of the Great Basin Experimental Range in 1912 generated a variety of range and watershed research within the Intermountain Region. The watershed management, effects of grazing on vegetative cover, and relationships of these to erosive flooding from high intensity summer storms as well as revegetation trials by vegetative cuttings and seeds on areas that had been depleted by overgrazing were documented and provided impetus to further research and management activities by land managers and researchers.

038. Ellison, Lincoln. 1942. Overlays as a visual aid in analysis of permanent quadrat records. Ecology 23(4): 482-484.

Overlays are useful in analysis because they simplify and, at the same time, preserve the pictorial value of quadrat charts. In using them, the ecologist is freed from a burden of irrelevant details, particularly those arising from variations in field methods, and is enabled to devote full attention to his essential task. The principal values of overlays are four: they assist in detecting general trends; they help account for puzzling fluctuations resulting from variation in method; they help correct omissions from the original charts and field errors in identification; and they facilitate study of the history of individual plants. Permanent quadrat records are an important data repository for the Great Basin Experimental Range.

Lincoln Ellison

039. Ellison, Lincoln. 1943. What is range improvement? The Ames Forester 21: 15-22.

The term "range improvement" is used very freely, but it is seldom defined. The term might appear to be so easily understood as to make definition unnecessary, yet its great variation in significance, as used by range managers, makes clear that the term means different things to different people. Perhaps the most unquestionable evidence of improvement is considered to be the appearance of species higher in the normal succession and the disappearance of species representing lower stages. Improvement of the soil is referred to rather incidentally, for if improvement of the soil is considered at all, it is generally assumed to accompany improvement of the vegetation, which is not necessarily true. Broad-scale ecological studies show that the two processes, soil formation and the development of vegetation, are interdependent, and that over centuries a deep soil will develop from raw parent material. The two processes are so interlocked in complexity that each is both an effect and a cause of the other. There is no reason to believe that the two processes may seem to be independent for short periods. An example from the Wasatch Plateau of the Great Basin Experimental Range makes the point. A m^2 quadrat compared in 1919 and

USDA Forest Service Gen. Tech. Rep. RMRS-GTR-305WWW. 2013

20

1940 showed the predominant *Achillea* had changed to *Agropyron* and the number of plant shoots and biomass had increased by orders of magnitude. However the soil surface remained unstable and even degraded. Judging by the biomass and type of plant present in 1940, the range had "improved." There is a paradox: improvement of vegetation quality but depletion of soil continues—two antagonistic processes occurring side by side. How is this paradox to be explained? Succession cannot be explained so simply, it is more complex; some important problems of range research and range management are for future research.

040. Ellison, Lincoln. 1946. The pocket gopher in relation to soil erosion on mountain range. Ecology 27(2): 101-114.

In what is considered to be a representative part of the subalpine zone of the Wasatch Plateau on the Great Basin Experimental Range in central Utah, annual displacement of soil to the surface by pocket gophers was found in 1941 to be at least 5 tons per acre and to cover 3.5 percent of the surface. The base population of pocket gophers is estimated to be somewhere between 4 and 16 animals per acre. Most pocket-gopher activity is confined to herbaceous vegetal types where, as a result of grazing, the disturbed soil is most liable to exposure to the elements. Gopher diggings are absent within areas of spruce-fir timber. There is a tendency for gopher diggings to be cast out into bare spaces between masses of vegetation where the loose soil is most exposed to atmospheric influences and consequent erosion. There is a similar tendency for gopher diggings to be concentrated in gullies where the soil is readily swept away by spring runoff and runoff from summer storms. Both these effects are pronounced in proportion as range is depleted; on range in good condition, where the cover is not patchy but practically complete, and where gullies are absent, they are relatively unimportant. The tendency for the pocket gopher to displace soil consistently downhill is one factor in normal erosional creep, and its magnitude is abnormally increased in proportion as protective vegetation is absent. No evidence has been found on the Wasatch Plateau that tunnels of pocket gophers concentrate overland flow in a degree to create gullies, unless, possibly, abnormal surficial runoff is induced by other causes. Delayed infiltration, the cause of gully-cutting runoff, cannot be attributed to pocket-gopher activities. On the contrary, loosening of soil and formation of minor irregularities on the soil surface by pocket gophers no doubt increase rapidity of infiltration. No evidence has been found on the Wasatch Plateau that pocket gophers destroy vegetation to a sufficient degree to cause accelerated erosion. Pocket-gopher diggings provide a surface for establishment of vegetation that is less favorable than an undisturbed soil surface with a vegetal cover, but apparently more favorable than a severely eroded surface. They seem to be instrumental in bringing about revegetation of some erosion-pavement areas. The pocket gopher is an agent in both geologic normal and in accelerated erosion. However, the pocket gopher is not the primary cause of accelerated erosion on the Wasatch Plateau. The primary cause of accelerated erosion is overgrazing. The amount of accelerated soil loss resulting from pocket gopher activity is related to the degree to which the soil mantle is dissected and the soil surface bared by man's abuse of the land.

041. Ellison, Lincoln. 1947. Subalpine vegetation of the Wasatch Plateau. Minneapolis and St. Paul, MN: University of Minnesota. 365 p. Dissertation.

The purpose of this study is to reconstruct the character of the original vegetation in the subalpine zone of the Wasatch Plateau in central Utah, which has been greatly modified since settlement, and to describe the changes that vegetation has undergone, primarily as a result of grazing by livestock. Even though great increases in vegetation have occurred in many parts of the subalpine zone during the last 40 years since grazing has been better regulated, the changes in vegetation on permanent quadrats during the past decade or two suggest that this upward trend has ceased. It appears, therefore, that management practices that succeed in raising the range from the lowest stage in secondary succession may still not be adequate for continuing improvement. It is clearly evident that losses of soil by accelerated erosion are continuing. Once well under way, accelerated erosion acquires a momentum that is increasingly difficult for vegetation to stop unaided. Stabilization of many slopes that have been eroding for years before all soil is lost, appears impossible, without artificial help. In considering changes in vegetation and soil, the process of accelerated erosion must be recognized as something distinct from succession. Accelerated soil erosion is not a successional process, or the converse of soil development: it is simply soil destruction. When the entire soil mantle has been stripped away, leaving only bedrock or erosion pavement, rapid improvement through secondary succession is no longer possible; the only possibility of improvement is by the painfully slow process of soil formation and primary succession. This work was performed, in part, on the Great Basin Experimental Range.

042. Ellison, Lincoln. 1948. Bettering management of Utah's range lands. Utah Magazine 10(9): 8-13, 25-27.

For the most part, the grazing lands of Utah are "wild" lands. They are the lands not suited to intensive agriculture because they cannot be irrigated, or because they are too rough, steep, or rocky to plow, or because their summer growing season is too short for cultivated crops. From the standpoint of area alone, they are the most important in Utah, making up well over four-fifths of the land area of the state. Although the rangelands of Utah are thought of as grazing lands for cattle, sheep, and other domestic livestock they have other uses and yield other benefits to man. Some are important for timber, many as watersheds, and all in some degree as habitats for wildlife. They are most widely used when they yield a maximum of these benefits in balanced proportion and in continuing supply. In referring to "grazing lands," therefore, it is primarily of forage values that are of primary consideration, but with other human values, practical and esthetic, always in mind. Range management research is multifaceted. Part of its effort is devoted to mountainous summer ranges, part to foothill and valley spring-fall ranges, and part to desert winter ranges. Studies are being carried out on big game as well as livestock range use. Many of these studies are cooperative with other persons or agencies. On winter range studies, private individuals and the U.S. Bureau of Land Management cooperate; on spring-fall range studies, the Bureau of Animal Industry; on big game-livestock studies, Utah State Fish and Game Commission,

USDA Forest Service Gen. Tech. Rep. RMRS-GTR-305WWW. 2013

22

Utah State Agricultural College and Experiment Station, U.S. Fish and Wildlife Service, and U.S. Bureau of Land Management. Range management problems, in other words, are being attacked on a wide front, on many kinds of lands. The research results apply, therefore, to land in all kinds of ownership, Federal, state and private. Observations and research results leading to this review were obtained, in part, from the Great Basin Experimental Range.

043. Ellison, Lincoln. 1949. Establishment of vegetation on depleted subalpine range as influenced by microenvironment. Ecological Monographs 19(2): 95-121.

This paper deals primarily with certain depleted plant communities of the subalpine upland-herb association of the Wasatch Plateau in central Utah. Here much of the original herbaceous vegetation was destroyed by overgrazing years ago. Widespread soil erosion, less severe today than formerly, but still occurring, is the rule rather than the exception. Reinvasion of vegetation has been strongly influenced by grazing pressure and erosion. Only a small proportion of the area of herbaceous uplands in the subalpine zone has yet had its soil adequately stabilized by vegetation. Permanent plot records show that soil surfaces that are essentially bare of perennial vegetation may persist in that condition for many years. At the same time, adjacent surfaces covered with a growth of dense, rhizomatous vegetation, particularly *Penstemon rydbergii*, maintain their identity, and under some conditions change very little in appearance, over similarly long periods. A corollary of this observation is that new plants of other species tend for the most part to become established within the *Penstemon* patches, not in the bare spaces where they are most needed for soil protection. Other rhizomatous species, *Achillea lanulosa*, *Artemisia discolor, Erigeron ursinus*, and *Aster foliaceus* form similar, though less persistent, patches, and harbor seedlings of later invaders. Evidence of association between new plants and established vegetation may be observed rather generally. A number of transects and permanent quadrats in depleted upland-herb communities are described for illustration. A similar tendency is observed in the low-shrub community in the subalpine zone dominated by *Chrysothamnus viscidiflorus*. The community spreads to eroding land by the establishment of young *Chrysothamnus* plants in tufts of *Stipa lettermani*. Essentially similar observations are reported from the oakbrush zone of the Wasatch Plateau, and the subalpine zones of the Aquarius Plateau and Wallowa Mountains. Planting experiments in the subalpine zone of the Wasatch Plateau corroborate these observations. *Agropyron trachycaulum* was planted within patches of Penstemon, at edges of patches, and in adjacent, relatively bare openings. Survival of grass seedlings was greatest inside patches of *Penstemon*, least in openings. Intensity in degree of association varies. Most species show a tendency for positive association, but with some species no such tendency is shown (e.g. *Stellaria*); with some others, negative association or dissociation may be detected (e.g. *Viola*). It is unfortunate for the land that those species that show dissociation most strongly, and grow in the openings more than any others, are generally ephemeral in character and least effective as cover. Intensity of association also varies with character of season, as shown by permanent quadrat records. A correlated observation is that the more severe the site, in terms of instability and physical condition of the surface soil, the stronger the tendency for association. Intensity of association appears to vary directly, too, with intensity of grazing and trampling by livestock. Among biotic factors that might be considered responsible for the presence of new plants in patches of established vegetation and their absence in openings, grazing animals are certainly important. Heavy grazing and trampling were what originally denuded the herbaceous uplands of the Wasatch Plateau. While grazing animals help to maintain the patchiness of vegetation, they are not more than a contributing cause to the phenomenon of association described in this paper. Those associations are demonstrated, both by observation and experiment, where livestock have been excluded. Subterranean foraging by pocket gophers may be a factor, and probably the tendency of pocket gophers to disturb more soil in openings than in patches of densely rhizomatous vegetation helps to keep the openings bare. Yet in places where pocket-gopher activity was not evident, seedling survival was still relatively low in openings. So far as edaphic factors are concerned, there appear to be no inherent differences in the soil of vegetal patches and openings. The soils are different, physically and chemically, and the difference results from the presence of established vegetation in one place in contrast to its absence in another. These differences probably influence association, but they are not decisive, for the same denuded soil experimental plantings under shade gave much better results than in the open. These plantings also rule out the possibility that chemical growth substances, which might be given off by established vegetation, are responsible for association. The planting experiments confirm a conclusion toward which observational evidence points. This is that moisture at and near the soil surface, together with soil instability are the most important factors in explaining association of new plants with established vegetation and absence of new plants in openings. Temperature is less extreme under vegetation than in the open, and frost heaving of the soil is less common. Moisture in the surface soil persists longer under vegetation than in the open. In short, from the standpoint of a seedling plant, the water balance in openings is less favorable than under established vegetation. Demonstrable association leads to the conclusion that the favorable influence of vegetation on microenvironment outweighs its influence in competition, which presumably is greater within established vegetation than away from it. Observed association, therefore, appears to be a resultant of two opposed forces or factor complexes. This conclusion is supported by the observation that association is more marked as the surface of exposed bare spaces is more eroded, or more unstable, or as current rainfall is more deficient. A range-watershed manager is concerned with bringing about restoration of vegetal cover as quickly as possible. The observations reported in this paper indicate that he should regulate grazing so as to provide, through the influence of vegetation already on the ground, the best possible microenvironment for establishing new plants. This work was performed, in part, on the Great Basin Experimental Range.

044. Ellison, Lincoln. 1949. The ecological basis for judging condition and trend on mountain range land. Journal of Forestry 47(10): 786-795.

USDA Forest Service Gen. Tech. Rep. RMRS-GTR-305WWW. 2013

24

Accurate judgment of range condition and trend on mountain rangeland of the West is no cut-and-dried matter. This fact is highlighted by a tendency toward increasing conservatism in grazing-capacity estimates over the years. Recently there have been sharp disagreements about proper management practices between livestock operators and officials responsible for management of public lands, and, in some instances, by wide differences of opinion among range managers themselves. A better understanding of the ecology of mountain rangeland is needed to help reduce these differences. This paper attempts to fill this need to the extent of explaining the ecological basis of the concepts condition and trend. It is written from the experience of more than a decade of ecological research on subalpine range-watershed lands in central Utah. Several conclusions have been drawn: (1) Since the range is a complex of closely interrelated parts normally in essential balance with one another, a standard of integrity should be provided against which range condition may be judged. (2) As a result of these interrelationships and because of the reactions of plants and animals on the environment, orderly change (primary succession) takes place without loss of integrity in the complex—this change is much too slow to be manipulated practically by the land manager. (3) Secondary successions result from disturbance of the complex but, by definition, accompanying long-continued soil erosion is not considered successional. Secondary successions are much more rapid than primary successions, and are capable of being manipulated by the land manager so as to produce desired results within a reasonable time. (4) When disturbance is so extreme as to destroy integrity in the complex, as evidenced by accelerated erosion, the terms *succession*—which should imply an integrated complex is no longer appropriate—and *destructive change* are applied in its place. (5) Range condition must be judged on the basis of the normal potential of the site. What this normal potential is can be ascertained most practicably by comparison with natural areas that have never been grazed. (6) While condition on eroded but now stabilized soils properly requires new standards, the closest approximations now available are research natural areas. (7) In judgment of range condition, soil stability is paramount in importance; forage values are secondary. Where soil is eroding, conditions are unsatisfactory. Where soil is stable, conditions may be satisfactory or unsatisfactory, depending on the desirableness of the vegetation in relation to the management objectives. (8) Where soil is eroding at an accelerated rate, the trend is downward. Improvement while soil is eroding is very nearly a logical impossibility and, from a practical standpoint, so is judging range trend. (9) Trend where soil is stable may be either upward or downward. It is to be judged by evidence of change in vegetal composition toward dominance either by more desirable or less desirable species. Observations and research results leading to this review were obtained, in part, from the Great Basin Experimental Range.

045. Ellison, Lincoln. 1954. Subalpine vegetation of the Wasatch Plateau, Utah. Ecological Monographs 24(2): 89-184.

The purposes of this study are to reconstruct the character of the original vegetation in the subalpine zone of the Wasatch Plateau in central Utah, which has been greatly modified since settlement, and to describe the changes it has undergone

USDA Forest Service Gen. Tech. Rep. RMRS-GTR-305WWW. 2013

25

as a result of grazing by livestock. Most attention is given the herbaceous vegetation of dry and mesic sites. To understand this vegetation it has been necessary to work out the salient characteristics of soil development and primary succession. The principal communities examined were (1) forb-dominated communities on cattle range, (2) grass-dominated communities on sheep range, (3) low-shrub communities, (4) communities of ephemeral species, and (5) erosion-pavement communities. Even though great increases in vegetation have occurred in many parts of the subalpine zone during the last 40 years since grazing has been better regulated, the changes in vegetation on permanent quadrats during the past decade or two suggest that this upward trend has ceased. It appears, therefore, that management practices that succeed in raising the range from the lowest stage in secondary succession may still not be adequate for continuing improvement. It is clearly evident that losses of soil by accelerated erosion are continuing. Once well under way, accelerated erosion acquires a momentum that is increasingly difficult for vegetation to stop unaided. Stabilization of many slopes that have been eroding for years appears impossible without artificial help. In considering changes in vegetation and soil, the process of accelerated erosion must be recognized as something distinct from succession. Accelerated soil erosion is not a successional process, the converse of soil development; it is simply soil destruction. When the entire soil mantle has been stripped away, leaving only bedrock or erosion pavement, rapid improvement through secondary succession is no longer possible; the only possibility of improvement is by the painfully slow process of soil formation and primary succession. Observations and research results presented in this article were obtained, in part, from the Great Basin Experimental Range.

046. Ellison, Lincoln. 1959. Role of plant succession in range improvement. In: Grasslands. Washington, DC: American Association for the Advancement of Science: 307-321.

This review article draws, in part, on experience and observations at the Great Basin Experimental Range. A central question is how it is possible to maintain a high level of range productivity under grazing with secondary plant succession. Logic argues that productivity cannot be maintained because depletion, as a result of selective grazing, appears to have no end and because most of the claimed benefits of grazing are unconvincing. On the other hand, experience argues that productivity can be maintained because of examples of range improvement under grazing and because of the persistence of palatable plants on natural ranges where they have been grazed by wild animals over many thousands of years. The answer appears to lie in consideration of the response of vegetation to its total environment. Range plant composition and productivity are determined in part by grazing pressure. Other factors, such as recurrent drought and interactions between plant species, may be just as or more important. Some species that are severely handicapped and reduced by heavy grazing are otherwise well adapted to the environment. In the course of succession under grazing, their place is commonly taken by opportunists that are unpalatable or that by other means escape the handicap of heavy grazing. When grazing pressure is lightened, at least some of the more palatable members of the original vegetation are able to reassert themselves, and other factors, such as the

USDA Forest Service Gen. Tech. Rep. RMRS-GTR-305WWW. 2013

26

competition of these species, reduce the opportunists. It is probably too much to say that pristine vegetation can be maintained under livestock grazing. Experience is generally showing, nevertheless, that a level of productivity much closer to the pristine can be maintained than has previously been supposed possible.

047. Ellison, Lincoln. 1960. Influence of grazing on plant succession of rangelands. Botanical Review 26(1): 1-78.

This review article draws, in part, on experience and observations at the Great Basin Experimental Range. Succession is commonly thought of as a constructive process; the origins of the word suggest growth and progress. In primary succession the development of soil with its contained organisms, including the complex vegetation it supports, is certainly a constructive process. Most of the familiar forms of secondary succession are also constructive in character. In contrast, secondary successions resulting from grazing are commonly thought of as being other than constructive. There are enough examples of severe overgrazing of range vegetation that it is generally known that reduction of plant cover by overgrazing leads to accelerated soil erosion by wind or water. Even if grazing changes the character of the vegetation without reducing cover sufficiently to cause erosion, the change is usually toward vegetation that is less palatable to the grazing animal and somewhat less productive. Various benefits conferred by grazing animals on vegetation have been suggested: (1) cropping may stimulate herbage production; (2) grazing may help a plant endure drought by reducing the area of its transpiring surface; (3) grazing, by removing some of the herbage, lessens the amount of mulch and thus, by encouraging early spring growth, increases production; (4) grazing animals carry the seeds of forage species from place to place; (5) trampling helps plant seeds of forage species; (6) livestock trails check the overland flow of water and thus encourage infiltration; (7) grazing animals fertilize the range. Taken in total, these presumed contributions of grazing animals to the welfare of range vegetation are not impressive. The benefits of grazing, if any, would appear to accrue to the ecosystem, to the range as a whole, instead of to the palatable species of plants that are grazed most.

048. Ellison, Lincoln; Aldous, C. M. 1952. Influence of pocket gophers on vegetation of subalpine grassland in central Utah. Ecology 33(2): 177-186.

Half of a 4-acre fenced plot in the subalpine zone on the Great Basin Experimental Range of the Wasatch Plateau has been systematically trapped since 1942 to free it from pocket gophers. Pocket gophers in the other half have not been disturbed. Weight of vegetation has been estimated three times: in 1942 before the effects of trapping could be felt, in 1944, and in 1950. At the initial trapping in the late summer of 1942 the gopher population was estimated to be 33 per acre, although some young may have dispersed by that time. Subsequent trapping twice yearly has reduced the adult gopher population from 23 on the 1.3-acre study area to a level between 2 and 8. Most of the gophers caught exert an influence on the "gophers absent" side only part of the year. It is believed that the gopher population on the "gophers present" side has increase since 1942. Results of trapping indicate that an average of 3.23 young are produced per pregnant female per year, that no more than one litter is produced per female per year, and there is a slight excess of males over females. Total production of vegetation (roughly half a ton of air-dry matter per acre) has not been greatly changed in 8 years of treatment. There is a slight tendency for total production to increase where gophers are present as compared with where they are absent. Common dandelion has decreased strongly where gophers are present and has increased where they are absent. This difference is attributed to foraging by gophers. Mountain dandelion, however, which also has fleshy taproots that might be supposed equally suitable as food, has not responded in the same way. Rhizomatous species, with the exception of yarrow, have increased where gophers are present as compared with their behavior on the area from which gophers have been removed. This is particularly true of sweetsage. Evidently species with established underground parts are able to take over bare areas and to grow especially vigorously where other vegetation has been removed by gophers disturbing the soil. Grasses and sedges tend to increase where gophers are present as compared with where they are absent. Most tall forbs have increased on both sides of the experimental area, and annuals and ephemerals have declined. These trends are probably the result of exclusion of livestock. Where pocket gophers are present, the soil is distinctly softer and looser than where they have been removed. It appears probable that gophers perform a useful function in loosening the soil, a function that seems particularly important in heavy clay soils subject to compaction under livestock grazing.

049. Ellison, Lincoln; Croft, A. R. 1944. Principles and indicators for judging condition and trend of high range-watersheds. Res. Pap. 6. Ogden, UT: U.S. Department of Agriculture, Forest Service, Intermountain Forest and Range Experiment Station. 65 p.

Management of mountain rangelands in the semiarid West, whether it be for forge or water, is largely range management. These lands not only function as producers of stream flow, which makes possible irrigation agriculture, but they also furnish summer grazing to large numbers of livestock. Both of these resources are essential to the economy of the West. Changes from the normal in grazing capacity or in stream flow characteristics on mountain lands are preceded by changes that occur in the soil and plant mantles as a result of grazing use. It is the job of the manager and of the user of these lands to recognize such changes in their early stages so that use may be adjusted and destructive changes averted. To be able to do this—to determine the conditions and trend of the range—is fundamental in range-watershed management. A careful appraisal of the elements making up mountain range and an analysis of the significance of the indicators used is needed to provide a sound basis in fact for judging condition and trend. This publication addresses these issues by characterizing high range-watersheds—typified by the Great Basin Experimental Range—through discussion of the biotic community, the soil, the climate, topography, and interrelationships between these components; by discussing change in the complex through exploring succession, change and balance, and change as a result of grazing; and by discussing standards of satisfactory range-watershed management including management objectives. The publication

USDA Forest Service Gen. Tech. Rep. RMRS-GTR-305WWW. 2013

28

also explores the concept of indicators by defining them and discussing the following indicators: litter, bare soil surface, observed movement of soil, soil remnants, accelerated erosion pavement, gullies, blowouts, wind deposits, alluvial deposits, species composition, age classes of species, roadside annuals, invasion of bare spaces, vegetation in gullies, patchy vegetation, accessibility of palatable species, relics, hedged shrubs, and current utilization. The procedures for judging range-watershed condition is explored by getting representative samples, observing and recording facts, and reasoning with indicators.

050. Ellison, Lincoln; Croft, A. R.; Bailey, Reed W. 1951. Indicators of condition and trend on high range-watersheds of the Intermountain Region. Agric. Handb. No. 19. Washington, DC: U.S. Department of Agriculture. 66 p.

High mountain lands of the Intermountain West have great significance and importance to its people, even though they make up only a small fraction of its total area. From these highlands, the accumulation of winter snow yields year-long stream flow, the lifeblood of the Intermountain country. They provide summer grazing for domestic herds and for wild game. They furnish timber for local sawmills. And finally, their forests, streams, and rugged landscape provide an opportunity for enjoyment and inspiration to all. The vegetation of these high mountain lands plays a particularly important role in regulating stream flow. Grasslands, brush fields, and forest hold the soil in place and keep it open and porous, so that even the most violent summer rains are safely absorbed. When the vegetal cover is intact, overland flow is virtually unknown. On the other hand, if the vegetal cover is greatly reduced, dashing rains wear away the soil, etching rills and gullies into the watershed slopes. In many years this deterioration of the upper slopes is reflected only in the sediment that collects in canals and reservoirs. But in those years when the most intense storms occur, the eroded slopes discharge the flood waters almost as fast as they fall. These pour down the gullies, uniting to gut the larger channels and finally, spewing mud and boulders out of the canyon mouth, wreaking havoc on whatever farm, dwelling, or town that may lie in their way. Judgment of condition and trend depends upon ability to recognize indicators and understand their significance. By proper interpretation of indicators, constructive changes in management may be planned, and on the same basis the effectiveness of management may be evaluated later. On the other hand, unless indicators of downward trend are recognized accurately and unless management is geared to correct the causes of downward trend, costly and even irreparable damage may be done to the range-watershed resource. This publication is intended to help the range manager judge condition and trend accurately in the course of range inspection. In order to make best use of the evidence on the ground, the manager has three major needs: first, a technical foundation of ecological principles underlying the concepts of condition and trend; second, an understanding of condition and trend as they relate to the normal and to objectives in management; and third, a knowledge of indicators of condition and trend, their meanings and their limitations. Observations and research results leading to this review were obtained, in part, from the Great Basin Experimental Range.

051. Ellison, Lincoln; Houston, Walter R. 1958. Production of herbaceous vegetation in openings and under canopies of western aspen. Ecology 39 (2): 337-345.

In order to evaluate the potential productivity of aspen openings and the ground vegetation under aspen, plots were established in openings and under aspen canopy at four sites that were seeded with *Bromus carinatus, Elymus glaucus, Rudbeckia occidentalis,* and *Heracleum lanaturn.* Yields at the end of the third season furnish the basis for this report. In order to evaluate the effect of root competition from aspen, paired sets of plots were trenched to cut the aspen roots. Plots in the open were much more productive than trenched plots under aspen, indicating that the potential for production in openings is greater than under aspen. (A complication was introduced by the fact that full stands were less consistently attained on the open plots than in aspen shade. This is believed to be a reflection of faulty technique rather than of inherently lower productivity in the open.) The most consistently successful species was *Bromus*; the least, *Heracleum.* The results of this study are confirmed by natural areas in which production of herbaceous vegetation in aspen openings appears to be greater than within the aspen stand. Trenched plots were much more productive than untrenched plots under aspen, which suggests that the principal factor in depressing yields under the aspen is root competition. These effects were still visible 3 years after trenching was discontinued. A tendency was noted for increased production with increasing altitude. This trend may be related to an estimated increase of 1 inch in summer (May through September) precipitation between the lowest and highest sites, and to warmer exposures at the upper two than at the lower two sites. The trend was noted on the trenched and, to a lesser extent, on the open plots, but in no case on the untrenched plots. This suggests that the environmental benefits associated with altitude (e.g., increased precipitation) are more readily taken advantage of by the trees than by their undergrowth. Utilization of forage by livestock is heavier in openings than under an aspen canopy. Throughout the aspen type, this difference in use intensity, together with the more adverse microclimatic effects associated with heavy grazing in openings, is believed to be responsible for the poorer production and species composition commonly noted in openings than under the aspen canopy. Relative production under aspen canopy and in adjacent openings can be used as an aid in judging range condition. The openings are "key" areas for management. Much of this research was performed on the Great Basin Experimental Range.

052. Forsling, C. L. 1924. Range studies as an aid to livestock production. The Producer 6(7): 3-6; 6(8): 8.

The first work in the development of methods of grazing to improve depleted range and handle sheep on the range was conducted on the national forests of eastern Oregon. After a few years in that region, the main activities were shifted to the Manti National Forest in central Utah, where the Great Basin Range Experiment Station was established in 1913. In 1915 the Jornada Range Experiment Station in southern New Mexico, and the Santa Rita Station in southern Arizona, were taken over by the Forest Service. These are the only three stations devoted entirely to the study of range management problems. Some of the more important projects that

USDA Forest Service Gen. Tech. Rep. RMRS-GTR-305WWW. 2013

30

have been worked on to date include: (1) proper degree of utilization of range forage; (2) proper season of use; (3) improvement of rangelands by artificial reseeding; (4) systems of grazing to obtain natural revegetation of the range; (5) methods of handling stock on the range; (6) increasing the calf crop; (7) reducing losses from various causes; and (8) water development.

053. Forsling, C. L. 1927. Making grazing lands more productive. National Wool Grower 17(6): 19-21, 44-46, 48.

The future of the grazing industry and of individual operators of that industry depends upon how well the productivity of grazing lands is maintained and how efficiently the feed produced is utilized. It is obvious that the industry cannot continue successfully unless an abundant supply of relatively cheap range feed is available. There are two main factors that have tended to make the grazing problems more acute: diminished area of range land and overgrazing and the subsequent decline in carrying capacity. When the West was first settled practically the entire land area was available for grazing. This is no longer the case since farming and other land uses have reduced the area available for grazing. More area is now required for the same number of stock than was previously required. These conditions tended to increase the demand for range that resulted in an increase in the price of land and the amount of feeding, and a decrease in the quality of the range. One avenue left for maintaining an ample supply of grazing is range management aimed at maintaining or increasing the productivity of the range area, and obtaining maximum use of the forage each year. Observations and research results leading to this review were obtained, in part, from the Great Basin Experimental Range.

054. Forsling, C. L. 1928. The soil protection problem. Journal of Forestry 26(8): 994-997.

Watershed protection may be separated into four main divisions: (1) protection of the water supply; (2) checking of floods; (3) checking of erosion to prevent the silting up of reservoirs and similar damage; and (4) checking of erosion to prevent depletion of the soil itself. Of these the fourth is the most far-reaching. The soil, after all, is the basic resource of the nation, since it is essential for the production of forage, timber, or farm crops. Observations and research results leading to this review were obtained, in part, from the Great Basin Experimental Range.

055. Forsling, C. L. 1928. The spring range problem. The Producer 10(5): 3-7.

Some of the early range studies imply that the difficulty might lie in too early use. Consequently, experiments were started to determine the effect of this early use, and to find out when grazing might safely begin in the spring and not cause undue injury to the range. These studies have shown that continued early grazing will do as much damage, and cause as much of a decline in carrying capacity as continued overgrazing. They have also shown that if grazing is delayed until the forage plants have made substantial growth in the spring, the range will hold up better and produce more forage than under the early use. For most mountain or foothill ranges, where bunchgrasses predominate, the important plants should reach a height of approximately 6 inches before grazing begins. This stage of development is usually reached about 4 weeks after growth begins in the spring. This period of unmolested growth will ordinarily be adequate also for ranges where the shorter grasses occur. The mere knowledge of the fact that grazing too early is injurious to the range does not in itself solve the spring-range problem. The fact that too early use is detrimental should be fully recognized in finding a solution. There appear to be three avenues of approach to the solution of the spring-range problem: (1) the application of range management to improve the grazing capacity of the available spring range now under control; (2) the establishment of improved permanent and temporary pastures for spring use; and (3) the administration of the public domain to make the suitable range available for exclusive spring and fall use. Observations and research results leading to this review were obtained, in part, from the Great Basin Experimental Range.

056. Forsling, C. L. 1931. A study of the influence of herbaceous plant cover on surface runoff and soil erosion in relation to grazing on the Wasatch Plateau in Utah. Tech. Bull. 220. Washington, DC: U.S. Department of Agriculture. 71 p.

This bulletin presents the results of a 15-year measurement of precipitation, surface run-off, and erosion from summer rains and a 7-year measurement of melted-snow run-off and erosion on two experimental watersheds, 11.244 acres and 8.972 acres, respectively, on the Great Basin Experimental Range of the Wasatch Plateau in central Utah. Summer run-off and erosion during 6 years on one of the watersheds when 16 percent of the surface was occupied by vegetation are compared with run-off and erosion on the same area during a later 6-year period when the vegetation occupied 40 percent of the surface, and with conditions on the second area where there was a stable 40 percent cover. The average annual precipitation on the areas studied was 29.51 inches. The results show the importance of herbaceous vegetation in reducing rainfall run-off and floods and in controlling erosion. They also show the need for regulating grazing to prevent depletion of the herbaceous cover on sloping lands subject to torrential rainfall.

057. Forsling, C. L. 1932. Erosion on uncultivated lands in the Intermountain region. Scientific Monthly 34(4): 311-321.

Since 1912, the research branch of the U.S. Forest Service has maintained a detailed study of the relation of vegetative cover and grazing to surface run-off and erosion at the Great Basin Branch Experiment Station (Great Basin Experimental Range) on the Ephraim Canyon watershed of the Manti National Forest. This is in a locality 10,000 feet above sea-level where the annual precipitation, more than two thirds of which is winter snow, is about 30 inches. Paired watersheds have been manipulated to demonstrate the importance of plant cover and grazing pressure on surface run-off and erosion and these variables.

058. Forsling, C. L.; Dayton, W. A. 1931. Artificial reseeding on western mountain range lands. Circular 178. Washington, DC: U.S. Department of Agriculture. 48 p.

USDA Forest Service Gen. Tech. Rep. RMRS-GTR-305WWW. 2013

32

Investigations and experience, including those on the Great Basin Experimental Range, indicate that reseeding will be successful on areas with rainfall, soil, and other growing conditions above the average. Such areas include mountain meadows, moist parks, alluvial bottoms along streams, and the more favorable slopes where the average annual precipitation is 17 inches or more, and where restoration of the native vegetation by range management is unpractical. Artificial reseeding cannot yet be made to take the place, on any considerable scale, of judicious grazing that will result in natural revegetation of depleted rangelands. In addition to the selection of the more favorable areas, the plants adapted to them, and the probability of restoring the native vegetation, other important considerations include the possibility of restricting grazing of the seeded species until they are well established; grazing the reseeded range where the forage crop will be maintained and the expense involved in reseeding will be offset within a reasonable period by increased income. Whenever artificial reseeding is undertaken with a species hitherto untried in any given locality, the operator, because of the many factors that enter in, should begin the work on a small scale or trial basis. Certain cultivated species such as common bromegrass, Kentucky and Canada bluegrass, timothy, orchard grass, and redtop have given very satisfactory results in reseeding. Some of the native western grasses, including the big mountain bromegrasses and several of the wheatgrasses, have given equally good results. Their use, however, is limited by the fact that the seed of all except slender wheatgrass may be procured only by collecting it on the range from naturally grown plants. Methods of treating the land for planting include trampling in the seed with sheep or cattle, harrowing the ground with a farm harrow or a wooden-peg harrow or brush drag constructed from materials available on the ground, plowing furrows at 3- to 4-foot intervals parallel to the contour of the land, and in some cases complete tillage by plowing and harrowing. Ordinarily, however, conditions will not justify an expenditure of more than $3.50 an acre for the complete operation, including cost of the seed; only under exceptionally favorable conditions is an outlay of as much as $6 per acre justified. This, on land of average productivity, excludes plowing and usually more than one harrowing. The best time to seed varies with climatic conditions. The most important consideration is that there should be an ample supply of soil moisture from the time of germination of the seed until seedlings have become well established and deeply enough rooted to withstand drought periods that may occur during the months of favorable growing temperatures. Where erosion of the soil is occurring as the result of depletion of the plant cover by overgrazing, fire, or other causes, artificial reseeding or planting to restore a plant cover will control the erosion. The methods to employ are much the same as in artificial reseeding to increase forage production, although a higher expense and a greater use of seed per acre are usually justified because of the greater values involved. Artificial reseeding, as a supplemental measure, sometimes lends itself to temporary conversion of cut-over timberlands to grazing purposes, pending restocking with tree reproduction as on Douglas fir lands in the Pacific Northwest, provided the seeding and grazing do not interfere with the establishment of tree reproduction. Seeding areas where poisonous plants have been eradicated by grubbing is often justified. Thus far, work in artificial reseeding on rangelands has been confined largely to cultivated species and a few native western range plants. There are still many undeveloped possibilities such as further trials with native range plants, the search in foreign countries for plants suited to western range conditions, and the development of more suitable forms by plant breeding and selection. The success with the few native western species tried, the successful introduction into the United States of many foreign species for other purposes, and breeding of cereals and other crop plants suggest that promising results will be attained as more attention is devoted to range forage plants.

059. Frischkneckt, Neil C. 1949. Seedling emergence and survival of sixteen grasses in central Utah. Logan, UT: Utah State University. 54 p. Thesis.

Because survival during the seedling stage is of vital importance to the establishment of grasses, a study of seedling emergence and survival was made of 16 grass species or strains planted in early-fall, late-fall, and spring at two sites in Central Utah: one in the sagebrush zone, and the other in the oakbrush zone. Seedling emergence from early-fall plantings, which began in the fall of 1947 and continued through the winter, was higher at both sites than emergence from late-fall and spring plantings in which seeds did not germinate until spring. There was great variability in seedling survival up to the second growing season between sites, and also between and within species, seasons of planting, and dates of seedling counts. The great differences in survival between the two sites is attributed principally to the drought, which took a heavy toll on seedlings in the sagebrush zone in the summer and fall of 1948. Differences as a result of winter mortality were less striking between the two sites. Mortality as a result of wintering was from three main courses at both sites: (1) heaving of seedlings due to the alternate freezing and thawing of the very wet soil surfaces; (2) breaking of the primary leaf near the ground level; and (3) unseen internal injury as a result of cold temperatures. Intermediate wheatgrass, mountain wildrye, and mountain bromegrass produced seed the first growing season from both fall plantings in the oakbrush zone, but showed stunted growth and showed no tendency toward culm elongation and production of seed heads from spring planting. Russian wildrye and orchard grass produced no seed culms for any season of planting. All other species and strains produced seed heads from all seasons of planting in the oakbrush zone. Mountain wildrye and intermediate wheatgrass were the only species to produce seed heads in the sagebrush zone, and these only from the two fall plantings. The research reported here was performed, in part, on the Great Basin Experimental Range.

060. Frischknecht, Neil C. 1951. Seedling emergence and survival of range grasses in central Utah. Agronomy Journal 43(4): 177-182.

A study of seedling emergence and survival was made of 16 grasses planted in early fall, late fall, and spring in the sagebrush and mountain brush zones in central Utah. Fall planting stimulated faster growth and development in intermediate wheatgrass, mountain brome, and mountain rye, causing them to flower and produce seed the first year in the mountain brush zone, whereas they did not flower from spring planting. The effects of fall planting were similar whether seeds germinated

USDA Forest Service Gen. Tech. Rep. RMRS-GTR-305WWW. 2013

34

in the fall or whether they lay in the ground over winter and germinated the following spring. The stimulation of faster early growth may be a factor contributing to higher summer survival of fall plantings in the sagebrush zone, but its extent or importance are not fully known. The research reported here was performed, in part, on the Great Basin Experimental Range.

061. Frischknecht, Neil C. 1959. Effects of presowing vernalization on survival and development of several grasses. Journal of Range Management 12(6): 280-286.

Fall planting or storage of soaked seed in a snowbank or refrigerator prior to spring planting accomplishes vernalization of some perennial grasses, notably intermediate wheatgrass and mountain rye. Other grasses used in this study, with the possible exception of Russian wildrye, are capable of first-year flowering from spring plantings without cold treatment, but it appeared that a higher percentage of plants flowered when seeds had been treated prior to spring planting; to what extent a few days' earlier emergence from treated seeds was a contributing factor is not known. The other species investigated were pubescent, tall, crested, and fairway wheatgrasses, Indian ricegrass and Great Basin wildrye. Whereas both snowbank and refrigerator storage effectively vernalized seeds, snowbank storage was advantageous in that it required no special equipment and seeds did not dry during the process. Use of plastic bags instead of cloth bags in the refrigerator lessened the problem of seeds' drying. These cold treatments hastened emergence from spring planting and aided survival on dry sites. With such treatment, spring plantings compared favorably with fall plantings. This study suggests that use of vernalized seed in spring planting of some range grasses may help obtain successful stands when fall planting has not been feasible. The research reported here was performed, in part, on the Great Basin Experimental Range.

062. Frischknecht, Neil C.; Plummer, A. Perry. 1949. A simplified technique for determining herbage production on range and pasture land. Agronomy Journal 41(2): 63-65.

The use of a 9.6 square foot plot is suggested primarily as a procedure for training to estimate herbage production directly in pounds per acre in the field. It has important added value in experimental work when it is desirable to make annual or seasonal checks on production. The use of this procedure in making forage inventories will fulfill a need for a method that is rapid, easy to use, and mechanically sound. The technique is recommended to range and pasture technicians who are concerned with measurement, maintenance, and improvement or forage resources. The research reported here was performed, in part, on the Great Basin Experimental Range.

063. Frischknecht, Neil C.; Plummer, A. Perry. 1955. A comparison of seeded grasses under grazing and protection on a mountain brush burn. Journal of Range Management 8(4): 170-175.

Twenty-two grass species were seeded on contour strips already established with smooth brome on a mountain brush site on the Great Basin Experimental Range in the fall of 1944. Two transects were established across all strips in 1946; one was fenced to exclude livestock grazing whereas the other has been grazed heavily by livestock each year since establishment until 1952. Only intermediate wheatgrass, pubescent wheatgrass, quackgrass and meadow brome maintained dominance to smooth brome under both heavy gazing and protection through the study. The increased yields of big sagebrush and snowberry on the grazed transect are associated with reduced grass vigor, and in the case of snowberry, perhaps with an added stimulative effect of grazing. In addition, many sagebrush seedlings appeared on the gazed transect beginning in 1951. In a burned area, six browse species (snowberry, Gambel oak, chokecherry, serviceberry, bigtooth maple, and horsebrush) sprouted readily from the crowns. Except for horsebrush, all provide good browse. Big sagebrush was killed by the fire.

064. Geary, Edward A. 1992. The proper edge of the sky, the high plateau country of Utah. Salt Lake City, UT: University of Utah Press. 282 p.

Attempts to restore the vegetation of the Wasatch Plateau has been a slow and difficult process, still not completed after more than a century. Even after livestock numbers were reduced, the denuded lands continued to spill mud and boulders into the valley with each summer storm. The most devastating floods in Sanpete history occurred in 1909, and the flood basins at the mouths of the canyons even yet have their uses. A significant chapter in the restoration process was the establishment of the Utah Experiment Station (later renamed the Great Basin Experiment Station and still later the Great Basin Experimental Range) in Ephraim Canyon in 1912, which brought the first true range scientists into the region. These scientists, such as Arthur W. Sampson, A. Perry Plummer, and Lincoln Ellison, deserve the title of pioneer as much as the first Sanpete settlers in 1849.

065. Gill, Richard A. 2007. Influence of 90 years of protection from grazing on plant and soil. Rangeland Ecology and Management 60(1): 88-98.

Human communities in the Intermountain West depend heavily on subalpine rangelands because of their importance in providing water for irrigation and forage for wildlife and livestock. In addition, many constituencies are looking to managed ecosystems to sequester carbon in plant biomass and soil C to reduce the impact of anthropogenic CO_2 on climate. This work builds on a 90-year-old grazing experiment in mountain meadows on the Wasatch Plateau in central Utah. The purpose of this study was to evaluate the influence of 90 years of protection from grazing on processes controlling the input, output, and storage of C in subalpine rangelands. Long-term grazing significantly reduced maximum biomass in all years compared with plots within grazing exclosures. For grazed plots, interannual variability in aboveground biomass was correlated with July precipitation and temperature ($R^2 = 0.51$), while there was a weak correlation between July precipitation and biomass in ungrazed plots ($R^2 = 0.24$). Livestock grazing had no statistically significant impacts on total soil C or particulate organic matter (POM), although grazing did increase active soil C and decrease soil moisture. Grazing significantly increased the proportion of total soil C pools that were potentially mineralizable in the laboratory, with soils from grazed plots evolving 4.6 percent of

USDA Forest Service Gen. Tech. Rep. RMRS-GTR-305WWW. 2013

36

total soil C in 1 year while ungrazed plots lost 3.3 percent of total soil C. Volumetric soil moisture was consistently higher in ungrazed plots than grazed plots. The changes in soil C chemistry may have implications for how these ecosystems will respond to forecast climate change. Because grazing has resulted in an accumulation of easily decomposable organic material, if temperatures warm and summer precipitation increases as is anticipated, these soils may become net sources of CO_2 to the atmosphere creating a positive feedback between climate change and atmospheric CO_2. The research reported here was performed, in part, on the Great Basin Experimental Range.

066. Godfrey, Andrew E. 1985. Prediction and protection for slope hazards, Utah's landslides of 1983 as a magnitude-frequency event with a finite return probability. In: Bowles, David S., editor. Delineation of landslide, flash flood, and debris flow hazards in Utah. Proceedings of a Specialty Conference: 1984 June 14-15; Logan, UT. General Series UWRL/G-85/03. Logan, UT: Utah State University, Utah Water Research Laboratory: 67-85.

Preliminary results from this study indicate that mass movements in the most unstable areas of the Wasatch Plateau, such as those underlain by the North Horn Formation, can occur with equal probability in any given year. However, the total land area involved is only a small percentage of the entire Wasatch Plateau. Examples of these landslides are the one in Bulger Canyon (1971), which involved 10 acres, and the one above Manti (1974) involving about 300 acres. In contrast, the wet year of 1983 produced a higher percentage of area involved in mass movement on the Wasatch Plateau, about 6,500 acres. In addition, the 1983 slides occurred in areas of lower landslide susceptibility than the areas involved in drier years. When viewed as magnitude-frequency events, the effects of mass movements in shaping landforms can be placed in proper perspective. Although the locations of specific slides cannot be predicted, since statistical analysis results in the loss of a degree of spatial resolution, these magnitude-frequency data, combined with gradational landslide hazard studies, enhance predictions of hazards to man-made structures. This research draws on experiences in the Great Basin Experimental Range (GBER); the GBER was affected by the 1983 landslides.

067. Grah, Oliver John. 1983. Spatial and temporal distribution of infiltration rates on a small subalpine watershed. Logan, UT: Utah State University. 186 p. Thesis.

Field studies were conducted to determine the spatial and temporal distribution of infiltration rates on a small subalpine watershed on the Great Basin Experimental Range in central Utah. Of particular interest was the distribution of infiltration rates relative to overland flow distance, elevation, total vegetal cover and soil bulk density. Infiltration readings were taken twelve times during the infiltration process at 120 sample points on a 0.45-hectare area. The Horton, modified Kostiakov and Philip infiltration models were statistically fitted to the observed infiltration rates. Infiltration variability was described by assigning the frequency distributions of each of the twelve infiltration rate data sets and by constructing semivariograms. Infiltration variability decreased from a high of 1 minute to a low at 55 minutes. One minute infiltration rates were found to be two parameters lognormally distributed; the other eleven infiltration data sets were found to be three parameter lognormally distributed as were long-time gravity terms of the three infiltration models. The infiltration models were fit to the observed infiltration with high significance and thus were found to adequately model the point infiltration process. The long time gravity terms of the infiltration models were found to be highly correlated with the observed 55 minute infiltration rates. The significance level of correlation between observed infiltration rates and overland flow distance was found to increase from early time infiltration to later time infiltration as did the correlations between observed infiltration rates and elevation. Correlations between the twelve times of infiltration and total vegetal cover remained at a constant high value of significance as did the correlations between observed infiltration rates and surface soil bulk density. Semivariance analysis and the use of semivariograms revealed that the range, or zone of influence, increased from a low of 2.38 for one-minute infiltration to a high of 17.37 meters for 55-minute infiltration. A highly significant exponential relationship between range and time of infiltration was found. This indicates that infiltration is spatially heterogeneous at early times and more homogeneous at later times during the infiltration process across the study watershed.

068. Griswold, Sylvia M. 1936. Effect of alternate moistening and drying on germination of seeds. Botanical Gazette 98(10): 242-269.

The seeds used in this study include 9 grass, 26 herb, and 7 woody species of Utah range plants. Twenty-three of the 42 species studied gave little or no germination at temperatures of 22 to 29 °C. Other conditions must be used for them before the effect of alternate moistening and drying can satisfactorily be determined. The effect of alternate moistening and drying on the germination of seeds varies with the individual species. Of the 19 species that germinated at 22 to 29 °C, alternate moistening and drying had little effect on the germination of *Bromus polyanthus* but did increase the germination of *Stipa lettermani, Artemisia incompta, Lepidium densiflorum*, and *Plantago tweedyi*. This treatment slightly decreased the germination of *Geranium viscosissimum, Pseudocymopterus montanus, Chrysothamnus lanceolatus, and Stipa columbiana*. Rapid drying had little effect on the germination of *Poa interior, P. secunda*, and *Chenopodium album*, but increased the germination of *Achillea lanulosa, Androsace diffusa, Pentstemon rydbergi*, and *Rumex mexicanus;* in all of these species slow drying decreased the percentage of germination. Rapid drying decreased the germination of *Bromus anomalus, Lupinus parviflorus,* and *Rudbeckia occidentalis*, while slow drying increased the germination of *Rudbeckia occidentalis* but had little effect on *Bromus anomalus* and *Lupinus parviflorus*. Increased germination was usually accompanied by a hastening of the germinative process and decreased germination was accompanied by retardation. In five species, however, *Poa secunda, Androsace duffusa, Plantago tweedy, Rudbeckia occidentalis*, and *Rumex mexicanus,* retardation was followed by increased germination. Most of the seed lots used in this study were obtained from the Great Basin Experimental Range.

USDA Forest Service Gen. Tech. Rep. RMRS-GTR-305WWW. 2013

38

069. Hall, Marcus. 2001. Repairing mountains: restoration ecology, and wilderness in twentieth-century Utah. Environmental History 6(4): 584-610.

Most Utah residents at first assumed that spontaneous natural processes would restore the land. But they soon realized that their degraded mountainsides did not recuperate very much or very fast. On the Wasatch Plateau where the Great Basin Experimental Range was established, large areas of pine, spruce, and fir that were logged or burned out never did grow back but remained as sagebrush or alder fading into aspen. Herbaceous areas were grazed out and never recovered. Even after the Manti Forest Reserve was established over most of the Wasatch Plateau in 1903, when the Federal government first limited livestock grazing and timber cutting, subalpine vegetation did not recover as expected. When destructive flash floods continued to rush down from these mountains, sometimes more frequently than before, the Forest Service established a research station in one of the plateau's most flood-prone canyons. Opened in 1912, the Great Basin Experiment Station's central mission was to find effective ways to restore stability and productivity to the West's denuded mountain watersheds. Extending south from the southern peaks of the Wasatch Mountains, the Wasatch Plateau is slightly taller and broader than most other mountain ranges that cross Utah's deserts. From the occasional promontory on this rolling, 80-mile plateau, side-canyons wind down to the valley floors on either side, with the eastern drainages eventually joining the Colorado River, and the western drainages flowing towards evaporation in the Great Basin's great expanse. Because the Wasatch Plateau's western escarpment drops faster than the eastern side, so does each of its western canyons and so does the water that drains them. Where each of the dozen western canyons opens onto the broad Sanpete Valley, Mormon immigrants constructed villages; the larger settlements of Manti, Ephraim, and Mount Pleasant mark the larger creeks that have provided life, but after thunderstorms have sometimes unleashed death. The most dangerous floods in the American West resulted not from melting snow but from brief, summer downpours. Sheep and cattle ranchers in the West had long spoken of the range's historic abundance and the need to restore previous conditions. By the late nineteenth century, ranchers almost always compared a better past with a worse present. Even with better knowledge about the flora that had once grown on the Wasatch Plateau, GBER Director Lincoln Ellison revegetated with almost as many failures as had the first director Arthur Sampson. Ellison set out in 1938 to establish what used to grow on the mountain, but in 1954 he concluded that even if he could determine what once grew there, such plants would probably no longer survive and reproduce anyway. Ellison had come to think that the real problem lay in soil loss, not in species choice. Even if he could travel back a century in time to survey pre-grazing vegetation with transects and quadrats he doubted that this previous vegetation could be grown on transformed soils. For Ellison, successful revegetation required soil replacement. After Sampson determined that the Wasatch Plateau's soils could not be replaced, Ellison decided that even soil loss might not be prevented. After Sampson concluded that the best approach was to preserve the range through better grazing management, Ellison warned that even preservation of degraded land might be inadequate. Instead of full restoration, his realistic management strategy for many of Utah's mountains had become partial repair or rehabilitation. When managers spoke of "rehabilitating rather than" restoring the land, they had lowered their goals, no longer expecting to reproduce an undamaged range. After 10 years at the station, Sampson was already counseling that the best strategy in Ephraim Canyon was to save what was left, since much damage was irreparable. Although stockmen expect great things from artificial reseeding, he wrote, "the Forest Service should impress upon them the futility of such work and the need for conserving the natural vegetation." Permanent damage meant that even the introduction of hardy species, whether native or exotic, could never completely repair the land. At the station's 1939 management seminar, participants were informed dryly that" there seems to be no possibility of finding the 'wonder plant' which will grow without moisture and withstand extremely heavy utilization." By mid-century, Utah's deteriorating mountain lands required land doctors. Subalpine pastures such as those of the Wasatch Plateau were not just eroded and unproductive, they were unhealthy. A decade later, Station Director Perry Plummer explained that by helping to stabilize eroding soil, sagebrush acted as "white corpuscles" of the range by holding land in place despite absence of species that had been there previously. Even though Ellison suggested that there might be no cure for the land's failing health, he and his colleagues still searched for strong medicine. Having worked to heal the land as nature would heal it—by revegetating with historically accurate native plants or by constructing trenches that might catch moisture to grow plants and assist natural soil-building processes—Forest Service personnel occasionally resorted to more invasive treatments. In fact, while constructing a series of deep, precisely leveled contour trenches in the Wasatch Plateau during the early 1940s, the Forest Service saw themselves administering intensive care. University ecologist Walter Cottam believed that if one could restore wildness to grazing lands, one would grow more forage, prevent more floods, and display more beauty. Cottam spent much of his life wondering about the pre-grazing condition of Utah's land. Like Ellison, he believed that a stable climax vegetation existed before the arrival of Europeans and he searched the archives and the land itself for clues about how this past vegetation had been altered. Like Ellison he concluded that soil loss represented worse degradation than vegetation loss. When calling for the "rehabilitation of the land resources still left to us," Cottam hoped to bring back wildness rather than Wilderness. As an advocate of rehabilitation, Cottam sought to restore through wildness to recreate wildland. Yet for all their failures, restorationists in central Utah made real progress in finding better ways to live on the land. They showed biological successes, by identifying handsful of native and exotic species that could survive in denuded slopes to begin accumulating soil. They revealed technical successes by refining horticultural methods that could produce sizeable quantities of local seed for revegetation projects. Restorationists demonstrated the difficulty of rehabilitation of subalpine lands but provided evidence that improvement and management of less environmentally stressful areas might be more practical to undertake. Finally they revealed by their struggles that there were others before them who recognized degradation and sought out means to repair it; in fact, it may be more gratifying to realize that the Forest Service acknowledged damage in the land and sought to restore it, instead of merely preserving the damaged status quo.

USDA Forest Service Gen. Tech. Rep. RMRS-GTR-305WWW. 2013

40

070. Hall, Marcus. 2005. Earth repair: a transatlantic history of environmental restoration. Charlottesville, VA: University of Virginia Press. 310 p.

This book explores the answer to the question of environmental restoration: Which systems need restoring and to what states should they be restored? It offers the alternative to the usual narrative of humans disrupting and spoiling the earth by showing that those who believed in restoration did not always agree on what they wanted to restore, or how, or to what form. This is done by discussing the forms that restoration has taken over the past two hundred years in the Italian Alps and Utah's Wasatch Plateau including the Great Basin Experimental Range.

071. Hall, Marcus. 2005. Restoring Utah's Rockies. In: Hall, Marcus. Earth repair: transatlantic history of environmental restoration. Charlottesville, VA: University of Virginia Press: chapter 3: 92-130.

This chapter documents the degradation of the Wasatch Plateau, including the Great Basin Experimental Range (GBER), by livestock grazing that lead to catastrophic floods in the Sanpete Valley beginning in 1889. That led to establishment of the Manti National Forest and later what is now known as the Great Basin Experimental Range where causes of the floods were documented and revegetation techniques were developed and plant materials for use in revegetation were tested and monitored. The chapter reviews the successes and failures and the philosophical bases for the actions that researchers and land managers have taken on the GBER over the course of the 20th century.

072. Heyerdahl, Emily K.; Brown, Peter M.; Kitchen, Stanley, G.; Weber, Marc H. 2011. Multicentury fire and forest histories at nineteen sites in Utah and eastern Nevada. Gen. Tech. Rep. RMRS-GTR-261. Fort Collins, CO: U.S. Department of Agriculture, Forest Service, Rocky Mountain Research Station. 196 p.

This study provides site-specific fire and forest histories from Utah and eastern Nevada that can be used for land management or additional research. Fire scars and tree-recruitment dates across broad gradients in elevation and forest type at 13 sites in Utah, including the Great Basin Experimental Range, and one in eastern Nevada were systematically sampled to characterize spatial and temporal variation in historical fire regimes as well as forest structure and composition. Similar data was non-systematically collected at five additional sites in Utah. These 19 sites include a broad range of forest types (from pinyon-juniper woodlands to spruce-fir forests) and fire regime types. In this report, local-scale spatial and temporal variation with site-specific details of historical fire regimes and forests that will be useful for local natural resource and fire management of individual sites are considered. For each site, topography, chronologies of fire and tree recruitment, and properties derived from those chronologies such as time-averaged fire regime parameters (mean fire interval and fire severity) and changes in forest composition and structure that have occurred since the late 1800s are reported.

073. Houston, Walter R. 1952. A preliminary study of some factors affecting herbage production in the aspen type of central Utah. Salt Lake City, UT: University of Utah. 27 p. Thesis.

In central Utah on the Great Basin Experimental Range, plants growing in openings between the islands of aspen trees produced four times as much herbage with an average of two to three times as many leaves per plant as did plants grown on areas under the aspen canopy. Removing the effect of aspen root competition under the aspen canopy increased herbage production 3 times, average length of leaves 33 percent, and doubled the average number of leaves per plant; it also increased the differences in herbage production and number of leaves per plant between these areas under the canopy and the openings.

074. Houston, Walter R. 1954. A condition guide for aspen ranges of Utah, Nevada, southern Idaho, and western Wyoming. Res. Pap. 32. Ogden, UT: U.S. Department of Agriculture, Forest Service, Intermountain Forest and Range Experiment Station. 20 p.

Aspen, *Populus tremuloides* Michx., the most widespread deciduous tree of the western United States, is one of the most prominent features of its native, high mountain habitat. Its conspicuous, relatively pure and single-aged stands, vivid green foliage in summer, bright yellow leaves in autumn, and distinctive white trunks at any season—all set it apart from the conifers and shrub communities that may surround it. In Utah, Nevada, western Wyoming, and Idaho south of the Salmon River, the area of range dominated by aspen approximates 2,000,000 acres. The lower and upper elevational limits of the type rise from north to south, from approximately 5,500 and 8,000 feet in southern Idaho to 8,000 and 10,000 feet in southern Utah. The type usually occurs between the mountain brush or sagebrush on the lower side and the subalpine conifer on the upper. The type is important to the economy of the region. Since it is one of the largest and most productive of the montane types, it is extensively used as a summer range, both for livestock and big game. It makes a considerable contribution to the regulation of streamflow, is also used for recreation, and furnishes some timber products, principally excelsior. Although forage production on the aspen ranges throughout the region has been reduced far below its normally high potential, little soil erosion is apparent; and from many observations the indications are that these ranges probably could be more easily restored to their former condition than many of the adjacent ones. Because of the importance of aspen ranges for grazing, range managers are particularly interested in recognizing condition and trend on them. As a basis for grazing management plans, the range manager must know the productive potential of the type, how near a particular range is to this potential, and whether the range is changing toward or away from it. The purpose of this publication is to furnish a guide that will enable the range manager to determine the condition of most aspen-type ranges in the Intermountain region. Data and experiences obtained from the Great Basin Experimental Range were used in preparing this guide.

USDA Forest Service Gen. Tech. Rep. RMRS-GTR-305WWW. 2013

42

075. Jardine, James T. 1916. Improvement and management of native pastures in the West. In: USDA Yearbook of Agriculture. Washington, DC: Government Printing Office: 299-310.

This report draws on the authors experience and observations including that at the Great Basin Experimental Range. For many years in the West there was room for expansion of the range stock industry. Large areas of unused grazing lands awaited the coming of the stockman. Only part of the pasturage that nature had provided in such seeming abundance was utilized by the herds that grazed in the western country. But this is no longer the case. From the desert to the line of perpetual snow there is now little unused range. Grazing, too, has in most cases been unrestricted, with consequent injury to the forage growth. This has gone on until it is evident that, to maintain the production of even the present number of livestock under range industry, run-down ranges must be improved and an efficient system of native pasture management worked out. The following points will help improve the management of native pastures: (1) Avoid grazing any of the pasture while the ground is wet in spring and the principal forage plants are just beginning growth. (2) Limit the number of stock to what is believed the whole area will support, at least in good condition for feeders. (3) Apply the principles of deferred grazing as nearly as possible. (4) Control and distribute the stock by fences, well-distributed watering places, and salt troughs, to minimize handling, natural travel, or congregating in large herds. (5) Watch the vegetation on the area as a whole to find out whether the best forage plants are increasing or decreasing, and increase or decrease the number of stock as may be necessary to bring the pasture, or each compartment of it, to its maximum forage production

076. Johnson, Hyrum B. 1964. Changes in the vegetation of two restricted areas of the Wasatch Plateau as related to reduced grazing and complete protection. Provo, UT: Brigham Young University. 123 p. Thesis.

Early in the twentieth century vegetation studies were started on the Wasatch Plateau in central Utah. This study is a continuation of a portion of those studies and is concerned with the vegetation and soils inside and outside two livestock exclosures on Horseshoe Flat—one located in a *Penstemon-Achillea-Artemisia-Stipa* community and the other in a *Stipa-Chrysothamnus* community. Soils inside and outside the exclosures at each site are similar in depth, texture, hydrogen ion concentration, and organic matter content. The volume of soil macropores and the infiltration rate of water into the soil were found to be significantly reduced under grazing conditions at both study sites. The vegetation cover at the beginning of the study in 1915 was severely depleted due to abusive, uncontrolled livestock grazing that had occurred previous to that time. Since the study began, grazing has been under the direction of the U.S. Forest Service. Throughout the study period grazing pressure has steadily decreased due to reduction in livestock numbers and the number of days making up the summer grazing season. Changes in the vegetation have been determined by evaluating records that have been kept of the vegetation on permanent plots located inside and outside the exclosures at each site. The major species occurring on the sites have been present both inside and outside the exclosures through the study period. The vegetation cover in the rhizomatous forb-grass community became more dense both inside and outside the exclosures as the study period progressed. The greatest increase occurred during the first few years after grazing was restricted. In general, those species, that showed the greatest increases inside the exclosures, are more palatable to sheep than those that showed the greatest increases outside the exclosures. Trends for species at the site are reported. These exclosures are part of an extended set located, in part, on the Great Basin Experimental Range.

077. Johnston, Robert S.; Tew, Ronald K.; Doty, Robert D. 1969. Soil moisture depletion and estimated evapotranspiration on Utah mountain watersheds. Res. Pap. INT-67. Ogden, UT: U.S. Department of Agriculture, Forest Service, Intermountain Forest and Range Experiment Station. 13 p.

Soil moisture depletion was measured with a neutron moisture probe on 14 sites representing 10 vegetation types on mountain watersheds on the Great Basin Experimental Range in Utah. A water balance equation was used to estimate evapotranspiration (ET). Both soil moisture depletion and ET varied considerably between sites and from year to year. Aspen (*Populus tremuloides*) sprouts utilized from 0.48 to 4.50 inches less water from 6 feet of soil than mature aspen; Gambel oak (*Quercus gambelii*) sprouts utilized from 0.25 to 1.15 inches less water than mature oak. By converting aspen to grass, ET losses were reduced from 1.08 to 5.18 inches from the surface 6 feet of soil and up to 7.59 inches from a 9-foot soil depth.

078. Julander, Odell. 1968. Effect of clipping on herbage and flower stalk production of three summer range forbs. Journal of Range Management 21(2): 74-79.

This study performed on the Great Basin Experimental Range showed that unclipped forbs produced more herbage and flower stalks over a 10-year period than plants clipped 50, 75, and 90 percent. Herbage production by the plants clipped 75 and 90 percent decreased rapidly over the years and few mature seeds were produced after 3 or 4 years of treatment. *Ligusticum* and *Valerian* can apparently stand about 50 percent use each year, but *Geranium* should be grazed somewhat less.

079. Keck, Wendell M. 1972. Great Basin Station—Sixty years of progress in range and watershed research. Res. Pap. INT-118. Ogden, UT: U.S. Department of Agriculture, Forest Service, Intermountain Forest and Range Experiment Station. 48 p.

This review narrates briefly the history of the Great Basin Experimental Range from its establishment in 1912 as the Utah Experiment Station. It describes key problems in management of watershed and rangelands and the experiments devised to solve them, and indicates how results of this research have been applied in practice.

080. Keck, Wendell M. 1972. Great Basin Experiment Station completes 60 years. Journal of Range Management 25(3): 163-166.

The Great Basin Experimental Range in central Utah completed 60 years of continuous ecological research in 1972. Scientists at the experiment station have pioneered research in watershed management, range management, climatology, and plant ecology. The Great Basin Experimental Range will be the locale for the Society's summer tour for 1972.

081. Klade, Richard J. 2006. Building a research legacy, The Intermountain Station, 1911-1997. Gen. Tech. Rep. RMRS-GTR-184. Fort Collins, CO: U.S. Department of Agriculture, Forest Service, Rocky Mountain Research Station. 259 p.

This treatise includes highlights of the history of organizations that preceded formation of the Intermountain Forest and Range Experiment Station in 1954. It provides detailed accounts of Intermountain Station research and administrative accomplishments, some of the people who led activities, and changes in the organization from 1954 through 1997 when the Intermountain and Rocky Mountain Stations merged to become the Rocky Mountain Research Station. Many significant Station publications are indicated by title in the text, and the references list includes other publications that provide additional historic background on research programs and results including work at the Great Basin Experimental Range.

082. Klade, Richard J. 2006. Chapter 1, The trail we will follow. In: Klade, Richard J. 2006. Building a research legacy, The Intermountain Station, 1911-1997. Gen. Tech. Rep. RMRS-GTR-184. Fort Collins, CO: U.S. Department of Agriculture, Forest Service, Rocky Mountain Research Station: 1-6.

This chapter reviews the importance of the Great Basin Experimental Range (GBER) founded as the Utah Experiment Station and later known as the Great Basin Experiment Station in the subsequent establishment of the Intermountain Forest and Range Experiment Station in 1928. The GBER was established in 1912; it was the second of several coalescing units that were eventually organized in the Intermountain Forest and Range Experiment Station, which itself was later renamed the Intermountain Research Station and then merged with the Rocky Mountain Forest and Range Experiment Station to become the current Rocky Mountain Research Station.

083. Klade, Richard J. 2006. Chapter 4, Great Basin—early days. In: Klade, Richard J. 2006. Building a research legacy, The Intermountain Station, 1911-1997. Gen. Tech. Rep. RMRS-GTR-184. Fort Collins, CO: U.S. Department of Agriculture, Forest Service, Rocky Mountain Research Station: 21-29.

This chapter documents the establishment of what we now know as the Great Basin Experimental Range (GBER) though its iterations of the Utah Experiment Station and the Great Basin Experiment Station. It details how the site was chosen and staffed and how research priorities were established. The first Director, Arthur Sampson, became an eminent researcher and later a professor at the University of California, Berkeley. The first studies included effect of grazing on aspen reproduction, natural revegetation of seriously overgrazed lands, soil acidity related to artificial range reseeding, growth and yield of aspen, erosion and stream flow, and effect of grazing on water quality. Permanent exclosures to compare grazed and ungrazed areas were established. Other early researchers at the GBER included C. L. Forsling, Clarence Korstian, Fred Baker, and W. R. Chapline.

084. Klade, Richard J. 2006. Chapter 7, The Intermountain Station, 1928-1953. In: Klade, Richard J. 2006. Building a research legacy, The Intermountain Station, 1911-1997. Gen. Tech. Rep. RMRS-GTR-184. Fort Collins, CO: U.S. Department of Agriculture, Forest Service, Rocky Mountain Research Station: 55-74.

This chapter documents the establishment and results of paired Experimental Watersheds A and B in the Great Basin Experimental Range (GBER) where treatments, seeding, and grazing were manipulated and reversed over time so that conclusions about land protection from erosion could be clearly drawn.

085. Klade, Richard J. 2006. Chapter 10, Station growth, 1955-1971. In: Klade, Richard J. 2006. Building a research legacy, The Intermountain Station, 1911-1997. Gen. Tech. Rep. RMRS-GTR-184. Fort Collins, CO: U.S. Department of Agriculture, Forest Service, Rocky Mountain Research Station: 87-124.

This chapter documents the growth and culmination of plant materials testing, selection, and use for rehabilitation of disturbed landscapes at the Great Basin Experimental Range (GBER) at the time of the first Director, Arthur Sampson. The experiments were broadly expanded and extensively tested by A. Perry Plummer not only in the GBER but in many other sites. The bulletin *Restoring Big Game Range in Utah* was published in 1968 (see Plummer, Christensen, and Monsen 1967, 1968).

086. Klade, Richard J. 2006. Chapter 11, New approaches, 1971-1990. In: Klade, Richard J. 2006. Building a research legacy, The Intermountain Station, 1911-1997. Gen. Tech. Rep. RMRS-GTR-184. Fort Collins, CO: U.S. Department of Agriculture, Forest Service, Rocky Mountain Research Station: 129-206.

This chapter documents the physical toughness and athletic prowess of two early Great Basin Experimental Range researchers, Arthur Sampson and Ray Price. Sampson was a boxer, wrestler, and runner and Price was a football, track, baseball, and basketball star. They used their physical skills to perform difficult physical labor at the GBER. Other GBER activities documented in the chapter include the review of plant selection for disturbed land reclamation that had it's roots in early GBER activities, and the new role of the GBER as the Great Basin Environmental Center managed by Snow College but partnered by the Rocky Mountain Research Station and the Manti-La Sal National Forest. It

USDA Forest Service Gen. Tech. Rep. RMRS-GTR-305WWW. 2013

46

also includes vignettes on restoration of the Sampson exclosures in 1990 by volunteers and contributions of Paul Hansen, a biological technician who did research and maintenance work at the GBER for nearly 50 years as an employee and a volunteer in retirement.

087. Klade, Richard J. 2006. Appendix A, Pechanec remembers his early days in research. In: Klade, Richard J. 2006. Building a research legacy, The Intermountain Station, 1911-1997. Gen. Tech. Rep. RMRS-GTR-184. Fort Collins, CO: U.S. Department of Agriculture, Forest Service, Rocky Mountain Research Station: 248-249.

This appendix is a contribution by former Intermountain Station Director Joseph Pechanec. He recalls spending the summer of 1932 at the Great Basin Experimental Range mapping quadrats and browse plots and estimating plant density on major plots.

088. Klemmedson, James O.; Tiedemann, Arthur R. 1994. Soil and vegetation development in an abandoned sheep corral on degraded subalpine rangeland. Great Basin Naturalist 54(4): 301-312.

Vegetation and soils inside and outside an abandoned sheep corral on degraded subalpine range of the Wasatch Plateau were studied to determine the influence of approximately 37 years' use of the corral on soil and plant development. Vegetal and surface covers were estimated. Herbage, litter, and soils were sampled inside and outside the corral and analyzed for C_{org}, N, P, and S. Soil pH, bulk density, and CO_3-C also were measured. Storage (mass/unit area) of C_{org}, N, P, and S was determined for each component. Yield and vegetal composition were significantly affected inside the corral boundary. Herbage yield was 2.2 times greater, litter mass 16 times greater, foliar cover of grasses 2 times greater, and forb cover 70 percent lower inside than outside the corral. Cover of meadow barley (*Hordeum brachyan-therum*), a component of the pre-disturbance vegetation of the Wasatch Plateau, was nearly 12 times greater inside than outside the corral. These and other vegetal and cover differences reflect inside-outside differences in concentration, storage, and availability of soil C_{org}, N, P, and S. Concentrations of C_{org} and total and available N, P, and S were greater in the surface 5 cm of soil inside the corral. Available P inside the corral was much higher in all soil layers. Because of bulk density differences, storage was greater inside the corral only for C_{org} and N at 0-5 cm and for P at 5-15 cm. Lower soil pH inside the corral appears related to soil P distribution and CO_3-C storage. Results suggest a need to reexamine earlier conclusions that tall forbs are the climax dominants of the Wasatch summer range. This research bears on the Great Basin Experimental Range (GBER) plant succession schemes and was conducted on the fringe of the GBER territory.

089. Klemmedson, James O.; Tiedemann, Arthur R. 1998. Soil-vegetation relations of recovering subalpine range of the Wasatch Plateau. Great Basin Naturalist 58(4): 352-362.

On degraded subalpine range of the Wasatch Plateau, we examined the hypothesis that recovery of vegetation, as manifested by its composition and biomass yield, was related to soil phosphorus (P) and sulfur (S) status. Six topographic locations were sampled to determine the relationship among composition and yield of grasses and forbs, litter cover, and soil characteristics including rock cover, organic carbon (C_o), total N (Nt), available nitrogen (N_{av}), total phosphorus (P_t), organic P (P_o) inorganic P (P_i) total potassium (K), total S (S_t), and element ratios; aspect effects were also evaluated. An alternative hypothesis was that productive potential was a function of depth of soil remaining after the period of destructive grazing. Differences among locations were significant for all vegetal attributes and for all soil characteristics except total K and C_o. Aspect was significant only for forb yield and P_t. Regression coefficients for yield and percentage composition of grasses were always opposite in sign to those for forbs. Yield and composition of grasses and forbs as a group were oppositely and strongly related to soil element ratios of C_o/P_t, N_t/P_o, C_o/P_t, and C_o/S_t, but were not related to soil P_t or S_t. There was no clear support for acceptance of the hypothesis that soil P and/or S were major factors in recovery of this subalpine range after destructive grazing, Differences in regression coefficients and lower r values among species within grass and forb groups, than for the groups themselves, to soil variables are a reflection of species individuality. This indicated a need to examine soil/vegetation relationships at the species level. Percentage compositions of grasses and forbs were oppositely related to the depth of A + B horizon, lending support to acceptance of the alternative hypothesis. This research bears on the Great Basin Experimental Range (GBER) plant succession schemes and was conducted on the fringe of the GBER territory.

090. Korstian, Clarence F. 1921. Evaporation and soil moisture in relation to forest planting. Transactions of the Utah Academy of Sciences 2: 116-117.

With the great diversity of sites that are available throughout the Intermountain Region for forest planting, it has been difficult to select those upon which success is assured, especially toward the lower limits of tree growth in the chaparral or oak-brush zone, without knowledge of the relation of climate to plant growth. A detailed study of the evaporating power of the air and of the available soil moisture for a given site not only affords an expression of the water relations of the plants of that site but also considers the other factors. This problem is being studied intensively on the Ephraim Canyon watershed of the Manti National Forest in Sanpete County, Utah (Great Basin Experimental Range). During the last two growing seasons, the evaporating power of the air has been measured by means of the Livingston porous cup atmometer and soil samples were taken at 10-day intervals to show the march of soil moisture on the five important sites under study: (1) Manzanita (*Arctostaphyllos platyphylla*) association; (2) Wild apple (*Peraphyllum ramosissimum*) association; (3) Sagebrush (*Artemisia tridentata*) flat; (4) Sagebrush flat, denuded of all vegetation; (5) Oakbrush (*Quercus gambelii*) association. Empirical plantations of 201 western yellow pine (*Pinus ponderosa*) transplants were also established on each site. The march of the evaporating power of the air and of the soil moisture was illustrated graphically. The success of the western yellow pine plantations

USDA Forest Service Gen. Tech. Rep. RMRS-GTR-305WWW. 2013

48

does not correspond very closely with the evaporation intensity because the latter does not take into account the question of the available soil moisture. The results secured to date would indicate that a satisfactory expression of these factors could be indicated by the ratio of evaporation to soil moisture. The evaporating power of the air and the available soil moisture appear to be the chief physical factors in limiting the growth and development of plants in the chaparral zone.

091. Korstian, C. F. 1924. Density of cell sap in relation to environmental conditions in the Wasatch Mountains of Utah. Journal of Agricultural Research 28(9): 845-907.

The investigation of the density of the cell sap of a large number of plants common to the important forest types of the Wasatch Mountains has yielded results of direct application in forest research. It shows that sap density may be used as an index of site in correlating the great complex of environmental factors with the physiological responses of the plant. The concentration of the sap of a species is not constant. It may be influenced by any of the environmental conditions affecting transpiration, the products of photosynthesis, or the supply of available soil moisture. Osmotic pressure in plants is more rapidly changed by fluctuations in the moisture conditions of the site than by temperature or light. Because of the wide range of sites covered in this investigation and the general agreement with the results of studies by other investigators, the following biological principles have been confirmed: (1) Annual herbaceous plants that complete their life cycle before the critically dry part of the growing season, and are therefore not subject to drought conditions, have low sap densities. (2) The concentration of the sap of woody species is much higher than that of herbaceous species. (3) During the growing season the lowest sap densities occur in those forest types that are well supplied with available moisture, whose plants are best adapted to secure it, and in which the complex of conditions is most favorable to plant growth. On the other hand, the highest densities occur on the most adverse (dry or saline) sites. (4) In the winter considerable variation in sap density is encountered, amounting in some cases to complete reversals of the densities of the growing season, due to changes in the soluble contents of the plant cells. In the case of evergreen shrubs, the conversion of starch to sugars materially increases the density of the sap. (5) A thick leaf having a compact structure with a thick epidermis and cuticle tends toward a lower sap concentration through its reduction of water loss from the leaf. The presence of epidermal coverings and hairs on the leaves also yields lower sap densities. (6) Greater sap densities are generally found in the more drought-resistant species. This project was performed, in part, on the Great Basin Experimental Range.

092. Korstian, C. F.; Baker, F. S. 1925. Forest planting in the Intermountain Region. Department Bulletin No. 1264. Washington, DC: U.S. Department of Agriculture. 57 p.

Reforestation by direct seeding is impracticable in the Intermountain region. The planting of nursery-grown stock, on the other hand has been successful under favorable site conditions. The seed used in the nursery should have a high germinative energy and should be collected from trees of good form and development found in localities adjacent to the areas to be planted and having similar soil and climatic conditions. The seedlings and transplants should be given sufficient water to produce vigorous plants, but an excess should be avoided. Where necessary, protection should be afforded against intense sunlight, frost, and snow molding. Unusually heavy, calcareous clay soils should be avoided for nursery purposes. It is essential that the young tree, in order to become established when planted in the field, should be able to maintain a conservative balance between water absorption and water loss through transpiration. To accomplish this, the transplant must have a root system sufficiently long to reach into the soil strata that retain available moisture, even though prolonged dry periods, and sufficient extensive development of actively absorbing fibrous rootlets on the laterals to enable it to draw moisture from a large soil mass. In order to preclude excessive transpiration, the top must not be too large. The best time to plant any species in the Intermountain region is just as early in the spring following the disappearance of the snow as the soil can be worked. Growth of the stock must be retarded until after it is planted. The occurrence and development of native species growing on or adjacent to the site should largely govern the selection of species for the planting site. Native species have proved superior to exotics in every case tested. The native herbaceous and shrubby vegetation may be used as a further index. In western yellow pine and lodgepole pine, the best stock is 2-1 transplants; with Douglas fir and spruces, 3-1; or in the case of an exceptionally short-growing season the fourth year, 3-2 stock. Age class should be used as the criterion only in so far as it is indicative of the desirable qualities mentioned above. Artificial forestation is ultimately destined to occupy a more important place in the management of the national forests of the Intermountain region than at present. In this region, where agricultural development is primarily dependent on irrigation water derived almost altogether from national forest watersheds, watershed protection and water conservation through the equalization of stream flow are the primary objects to be achieved in forest planting, timber production on a commercial scale being of secondary importance. The best field for planting is in the high mountains, where relatively heavy stands can be grown that will have higher timber values as well as watershed protection values. Data and conclusions presented in this report were drawn, in part, from the Great Basin Experimental Range.

093. Laycock, W. A. 1969. Exclosures and natural areas on rangelands in Utah. Res. Pap. INT-62. Ogden, UT: U.S. Department of Agriculture, Forest Service, Intermountain Forest and Range Experiment Station. 44 p.

This report presents a listing of 529 areas in Utah that have received little or no use by domestic livestock. Areas are indexed by county, elevation, date established, vegetation type, and type of animal excluded. Locations are further described by section, township, and range; vegetation information is also given. The Great Basin Experimental Range is represented.

USDA Forest Service Gen. Tech. Rep. RMRS-GTR-305WWW. 2013

50

094. Lull, Howard W. 1949. Watershed condition and flood potential. Journal of Forestry 47(1): 45-48.

A method of computing the expected runoff from a flood-producing storm on the Ephraim Creek Watershed is described in detail. Control measures needed to prevent such floods are suggested. This watershed lies, in part, in the Great Basin Experimental Range.

095. Lull, Howard W.; Ellison, Lincoln. 1950. Precipitation in relation to altitude in central Utah. Ecology 31(3): 479-484.

Occupancy of arid lowlands of the western United States is greatly influenced by relatively abundant precipitation in the mountains. This precipitation supports forests and forage, important in the lowland economy, that cannot grow at low elevations. Most important of all, mountain precipitation is the chief source of water for agricultural, industrial, and domestic use; and civilization in most of the West would be impossible without it. Mountain precipitation has a sinister aspect, too, in that it may give rise to destructive floods following misuse and depletion of vegetal cover. The Wasatch Plateau, which reaches a maximum elevation of 11,282 feet, has a pronounced north and south trend. Precipitation records at four stations, ranging in elevation from 5,543 to 9,860 feet in Ephraim Canyon, on the west front of the Wasatch Plateau, are the basis for this paper. They cover the period 1934 to 1948 inclusive. Precipitation increases with elevation. The relation between precipitation and elevation is linear, as given by the equation (precipitation in inches, elevation in feet): $P = 0.000494\,E - 16.95$. A zone of maximum precipitation, formerly believed to occur at intermediate elevations in Ephraim Canyon, is shown to be nonexistent, and is ascribable to concentrations of precipitation at Headquarters (8,850 feet) by a high cliff, together with loss of catch at Alpine (10,100 feet) because of windiness. The yearly pattern of precipitation is that of a sine curve, with a broad crest in late winter (February to April), and broad trough in late summer (July to September). The influence of elevation on precipitation is most marked in winter, least marked in summer. This difference is associated with a difference of storm types, which are predominantly general in winter and local and erratic in occurrence in summer. Most of the data collected for this report were collected on the Great Basin Experimental Range.

096. Lull, H. W.; Orr, H. K. 1950. Induced snow drifting for water storage. Journal of Forestry 48(3): 179-181.

If water in the form of snowdrifts can be stored on watersheds some of the critical limitations of western irrigation agriculture may be overcome. The authors present the results of preliminary investigations on natural and artificial drifting of snow together with suggestions as to how induced drifting may improve the usefulness of runoff. Data from the Great Basin Experimental Range were important in drawing the conclusions of this report.

097. McArthur, E. Durant. 1992. In memoriam—A. Perry Plummer (1911-1991): teacher, naturalist, range scientist. Great Basin Naturalist 52(1): 1-10.

A. Perry Plummer died on October 3, 1991. His passing deserves comment because he was a man who made a difference in natural resource management and research in the Intermountain area. He spent his professional career (1936-1979) with the Intermountain Research Station (formerly the Intermountain Forest and Range Experiment Station) of the Forest Service, U.S. Department of Agriculture at duty stations in Utah near

Perry Plummer

Milford and in Ogden, Ephraim, and Provo. He was the scientist in charge (equal to a director) of the Great Basin Experimental Range for more than 30 years and as such conducted and managed many research activities there.

098. McArthur, E. Durant. 2001. The Shrub Sciences Laboratory at 25 years: retrospective and prospective. In: McArthur, E. Durant; Fairbanks, Daniel J., compilers. Shrubland ecosystem genetics and biodiversity: proceedings; 2000 June 13-15; Provo, UT. Proceedings RMRS-P-21. Ogden, UT: U.S. Department of Agriculture, Forest Service, Rocky Mountain Research Station: 3-41.

The Shrub Sciences Laboratory celebrated its 25th anniversary with the symposium documented by these proceedings and a ceremony honoring people instrumental in its establishment: Mr. A. Perry Plummer represented Forest Service Research and Development and Dr. Howard C. Stutz represented Brigham Young University. The laboratory came into being because of the research foundation in Western shrub ecosystems generated by USDA Forest Service researchers and their colleagues and the need to carry on programmatic research in vast Western shrublands. Since establishment of the laboratory, dozens of scientists and professionals with technical and clerical support have conducted shrubland ecosystem research and development centered on shrubland ecosystem ecology and experimental range management including the Great Basin Experimental Range; seed quality testing and production and seed and seedbed ecology and adaptation; genetic variation, population biology, and systematics and taxonomy; breeding systems, hybridization, and hybrid zones; rangeland rehabilitation and restoration; equipment development, and cultural care of wildland species; soil/plant interactions, pathology, entomology, and mycorrhizae; nutritive quality, palatability, and wildlife habitat; and invasive weeds and weed biology. A continuing robust research program is anticipated that will build on previous research accomplishments, and will especially emphasize genetic variation and plant material development, fire

USDA Forest Service Gen. Tech. Rep. RMRS-GTR-305WWW. 2013

52

susceptible ecosystems, invasive weed control and biology, and the ecology and restoration of ecosystems on the urban/wildland interface. Laboratory personnel and collaborators have published nearly 800 titles during the past quarter century.

099. McArthur, E. Durant. 2005. Appendix D: history of the Great Basin Station. In: Prevedel, David A.; McArthur, E. Durant; Johnson, Curtis M. Beginnings of range management: an anthology of the Sampson-Ellison photo plots (1913-2003) and a short history of the Great Basin Experiment Station. Gen. Tech. Rep. RMRS-GTR-154. Fort Collins, CO: U.S. Department of Agriculture, Forest Service, Rocky Mountain Research Station: 55-60.

This appendix documents the importance of research that has been conducted at the Great Basin Experimental Range and details the history of the facility including establishment, research programs including watershed studies, vegetation composition and dynamics studies, plant adaptation for revegetation and restoration of depleted and damaged rangelands and wildlands studies, plant phenology, vigor, and nutrition studies, and silvicultural studies. The contributions of many scientists and their lives with their families are reviewed as is the role of the GBER in education and training of scientists and others.

100. McArthur, E. Durant; Giunta, Bruce C.; Plummer, A. Perry. 1974. Shrubs for restoration of depleted ranges and disturbed areas. Utah Science 35(March): 28-33.

This review article makes the case for the use of shrubs in restoration of depleted habitats based on research that characterized shrub adaptation including soil, climatic, latitudinal, and ecological tolerances. Shrubs in the Sunflower, Rose, and Goosefoot families in particular are useful in restoration planting in the Intermountain area. Background research leading to this review draws on work performed at the Great Basin Experimental Range.

101. McArthur, E. Durant; Monsen, Stephen B. 1996. Great Basin Experimental Range. In: Schmidt, Wyman C.; Friede, Judy L.; comps. Experimental forests, ranges, and watersheds in the Northern Rocky Mountains: a compendium of outdoor laboratories in Utah, Idaho, and Montana. Gen. Tech. Rep. INT-GTR-334. Ogden, UT Forest Service, Intermountain Research Station: 23-28.

This contribution describes the setting, history, climate, soils, plant communities, examples of research, facilities, and location of the Great Basin Experimental Range. Data bases are also included (climate, vegetation, maps, photographs and publications).

102. McArthur, E. Durant; Monsen, Stephen B.; Stevens, Richard. 1999. Field trip report: shrubland ecotones. In: McArthur, E. Durant; Oster, W. Kent; Wambolt, Carl L., comps. Proceedings: shrubland ecotones; 1998 August 12-14, Ephraim, UT. Proceedings RMRS-P-11. Ogden, UT: U.S. Department of Agriculture, Forest Service, Rocky Mountain Research Station: 293-299.

The field trip was held on August 13, 1998, accompanied by beautiful weather. It featured visits to the Salt Creek big sagebrush (*Artemisia tridentata*) hybrid zone on the Uinta National Forest and the Great Basin Experimental Range on the Manti-La Sal National Forest. The eight stops afforded opportunities to see and better understand the structure and dynamics of several plant communities and ecotones as well as the sagebrush hybrid zone and to learn about past and ongoing research and management in these areas. The field trip facilitated discussion on how management practices affect communities and their interfaces or ecotones. This report documents the field trip and provides information for those who may visit the sites in the future.

103. McArthur, E. Durant; Pope, C. Lorenzo; Freeman, D. Carl. 1981. Chromosomal studies of subgenus *Tridentatae* of *Artemisia*: evidence for autopolyploidy. American Journal of Botany 68(5): 589-605.

The sagebrushes (subgenus *Tridentatae* of *Artemisia*—new combination presented in the text) are western North America's most widespread and populous shrub group. Chromosome counts from 120 populations, including some from the Great Basin Experimental Range, confirm the base chromosome number at $x = 9$ with numerous $2n = 2x = 18$ diploids and $2n = 4x = 36$ tetraploids. Few higher polyploids are known, and aneuploidy and supernumerary chromosomes are rare. All 11 *Tridentatae* species are now known cytologically. All but the narrowly endemic *A. argillosa* are known from at least three locations: *A. arbuscula* ($2n = 18, 36$), *A. bigelovii* ($2n = 18, 36$), *A. cana* ($2n = 18, 36$); *A. longiloba* ($2n = 18. 36$); *A. nova* ($2n = 18, 36$); *A. pygmaea* ($2n = 18, 36$); *A. rigida* (2n = 18, 36); *A. rothrockii* ($2n = 18, 36, 54$, ca. 72); *A. tridentata* (2n = 18, 36, 54), and *A. tripartita* (2n = 18, 36). The chromosome number of *A. argillosa*, reported here for the first time, is 2n = 36. Chromosome numbers of eight subspecies also have been determined. The subgenus is characterized by autopolyploidy as indicated by morphologically indistinguishable $2x$ and $4x$ plants, a few mixed ploidy populations, consistent formation of quadravalents in $4x$ PMCs, a relatively uniform $2x$ karyotype, and a $4x$ karyotype, which is approximately twice the $2x$ one. Karotypic differences, if they exist at all, are on a populational level rather a systematic taxonomic level. The *Tridentatae* have apparently rapidly differentiated in situ in North America under the stimulus of recurring aridic cycles since late Tertiary or early Quaternary. They likely derive from more primitive circumboreal stock originating from the Eurasian homeland of *Artemisia*. The differentiation forms of *Tridentatae* were seemingly achieved through genic rather than genomic means. Karyotypic analysis supports a position within *Tridentatae* of *A. rigida, A. bigelovii,* and *A. pygmaea*.

104. McCarty, Edward C. 1938. The relation of growth to the varying carbohydrate content in mountain brome. Tech. Bull. No. 598. Washington, DC: U.S. Department of Agriculture, U.S. Government Printing Office. 24 p.

A detailed field and laboratory study was made at the Great Basin Branch of the Intermountain Forest and Range Experiment Station (Great Basin Experimental Range) during the period 1932-1934, to determine the character of growth and the time and amount of carbohydrate food storage in mountain brome (*Bromus carinatus*), a highly palatable range forage grass native to a large part of western mountain rangelands. The experimental area is located at an elevation of 8,850 feet in Ephraim Canyon, Utah. Annual growth of mountain brome is cyclic in nature, owing in part to atmospheric temperatures and in part to the plant's reproductive processes. The growth cycle includes current seasonal growth of herbage, secondary herbage growth, and root growth. Annual herbage growth begins some 45 to 89 days before winter snow disappears. Secondary shoot growth follows the production of the current seasonal shoots and flower stalks. The general trend of the combined sugar and starch fractions is from low values during the formative stage of shoot development to high concentrations following current seasonal and secondary herbage growth. The starch values in both herbage and basal organs exceed the sugar values; their respective seasonal trends correspond to those of the combined sugar and starch fractions. The study leads to the conclusion that sugars and starches are the more potent of the stored carbohydrate foods. Conversely, the behavior of the acid-hydrolysable hemicelluloses suggests that this carbohydrate is employed largely, as structural material. Evidence from the study warrants the conclusion that relatively high concentration of sugars in the basal organs and in the newly developed shoots on mountain brome are associated with resistance to low temperature and are essential to winter survival of the plants.

105. McCarty, Edward C.; Price, Raymond. 1942. Growth and carbohydrate content of important mountain forage plants in central Utah as affected by clipping and grazing. Tech. Bull. No. 818. Washington, DC: U.S. Department of Agriculture, U.S. Government Printing Office. 51 p.

The findings of these studies of the growth and carbohydrate nutrition of two perennial range grasses and two broadleaf herbaceous range plants native to the Great Basin Experimental Range of the Wasatch Plateau in central Utah, under natural conditions and total protection, clipping, and cattle grazing, are of importance as a basis for conservation measures and wise grazing use on western mountain rangelands. Research results lead to the following conclusions: (1) Although presence of snow and influence of other adverse climatic elements make it necessary to utilize high mountain ranges during the summer season when the plants are growing and producing herbage, such grazing should be so coordinated with the critical growth and developmental stages of the principal perennial forage plants that the plants may assimilate and store sufficient plant foods to maintain growth and produce herbage for forage in subsequent years. (2) Critical periods in the life cycle of the plants studied, as measured by the carbohydrate reserves at the end of the growing seasons and yield and vigor of the plants are (a) from flower stalk formation (including seed ripening)—the active reproduction period; and (b) during the forepart of the normal carbohydrate-storage period, which in the mountains of Utah takes place during August and September. Grazing should be slackened during these periods. (3) Early grazing, when plants are 4 to 6 inches high, provided it is not too frequent, and grazing near the close of the growing season, when the herbage is dry or drying, appear to be the safer periods of use if grazing is to be restricted as to periods.

106. McGinnies, W. G. 1930. The value of physical factor measurements in range research. Ecology 11(4): 771-776.

The vegetation on a given area at a given time represents a summation of all the factors acting to produce it. Any change in any factor or factors that changes the total effect of all the factors will bring about a change in the vegetation. The individual factors on two areas with identical vegetation composition are not necessarily the same, but the sum will be. Where the summation is different on two areas an equal change in one factor in each may produce divergent results. This accounts for the divergent reaction of a given forage species to grazing under different environmental conditions. Successional changes are brought about largely by the building up of a developed environment on the physical environment, and reflect the interactions between plants and animals and the basic physical habitat. Grazing by rodents, game animals, and domestic stock is a normal factor in successional changes; the absence of grazing is abnormal. Under ordinary conditions found in the Rocky Mountain Region, each species under minimum precipitation conditions gives way when grazed, withstands grazing under optimum precipitation conditions, and moves into areas of greater precipitation as that habitat becomes more xeric with overgrazing. An exact knowledge of the basic physical environment and the developed biological environment is necessary before advance can be made in range investigations. Data and experience obtained at the Great Basin Experimental Range were important in the preparation of this article.

107. McGinnies, William J. 1959. The relationship of furrow depth to moisture content of soil and to seedling establishment on a range soil. Agronomy Journal 51(1): 13-14.

The use of furrows 2 to 4 inches deep significantly increased soil moisture available for seed germination on a range soil by reducing the rate of moisture loss. Seedling establishment was improved by using a 4-inch deep furrow. This research was performed at the Great Basin Experimental Range.

Great Basin Experimental Range Watersheds A and B

108. Meeuwig, Richard O. 1960. Watersheds A and B: a study of surface runoff and erosion in the subalpine zone of Central Utah. Journal of Forestry 58(6): 556-560.

Watersheds A and B, in the head of Ephraim Canyon in central Utah on the Great Basin Experimental Range, have been under continuous study since they were established in 1912 to provide information on the influence of herbaceous cover on surface runoff and erosion. This study, still in progress, has yielded information on surface runoff and erosion under a variety of herbaceous cover conditions. Among the many important facts learned from this long-term study are these: (1) Natural recovery of damaged watersheds proceeds very slowly under the particular soil and climatic conditions of this area (clay loam soils, high intensity summer storms, and variable plant cover). (2) Restoration treatments hasten recovery of damaged areas with an accompanying improvement in quality and quantity of forage production. (3) There is a minimum ground cover essential to the control of surface runoff and erosion.

109. Meeuwig, Richard O. 1965. Effects of seeding and grazing on infiltration capacity and soil stability of a subalpine range in central Utah. Journal of Range Management 18(4): 173-180.

Seven years after disking and seeding to grass, main effects were (1) decreased organic matter and capillary porosity in the surface soil; (2) greater soil bulk density; and (3) decreased plant and litter cover. Seeding did not significantly affect infiltration or soil stability. Grazing during the previous 4 years decreased plant and litter cover and non-capillary soil porosity, but increased capillary porosity in the surface soil and decreased infiltration and soil stability. This research was conducted on the Great Basin Experimental Range.

110. Meeuwig, Richard O. 1970. Sheet erosion on Intermountain summer ranges. Res. Pap. INT-85. Ogden, UT: U.S. Department of Agriculture, Forest Service, Intermountain Forest and Range Experiment Station. 25 p.

Simulated rain was applied to small plots on seven mountain rangeland sites in Utah, Idaho, and Montana. Multiple regression equations were developed for each site relating the resultant erosion to cover characteristics, soil properties, and slope gradient. The magnitude of erosion was found to depend primarily on the proportion of the soil surface protected from direct raindrop impact by plants, litter, and (in some cases) stone. Soil organic matter favored stability of fine-textured soils, but apparently increased erodibility of sandy soils. The regression equations are presented in tabular and nomographic form to aid the land manager in the assessment of potential sheet erosion on sites similar to those studied. Data from the Great Basin Experimental Range were used in this study.

111. Meuggler, Walter F; Campbell, Robert B., Jr. 1986. Aspen community types of Utah. Res. Pap. INT-362. Ogden, UT: U.S. Department of Agriculture, Forest Service, Intermountain Research Station. 69 p.

USDA Forest Service Gen. Tech. Rep. RMRS-GTR-305WWW. 2013

57

A vegetation classification for the aspen-dominated forest of Utah is based upon existing community structure and plant species composition. Included are 36 community types that occur within six cover type categories. A diagnostic key using indicator species facilitates field identification of the community types. Vegetational composition, productivity, and successional status are included. Tables provide detailed comparisons of community types. The classification and descriptions are based on data from over 1,200 aspen stands scattered across the six National Forests within Utah including the Great Basin Experimental Range of the Manti-La Sal National Forest.

112. Monsen, Stephen B. 2004. History of range and wildlife habitat restoration in the Intermountain West. In: Monsen, Stephen B.; Stevens, Richard; Shaw, Nancy L. comps. Restoring western ranges and wildlands. Gen. Tech. Rep. RMRS GTR-136. Fort Collins, CO: U.S. Department of Agriculture, Forest Service, Rocky Mountain Research Station: 1-5.

This review highlights the contributions of the Great Basin Experimental Range to the broader context of range and wildlife habitat restoration in the Intermountain West. Much foundational research on range and habitat restoration was started or gained traction at the Great Basin Experimental Range.

113. Monsen, Stephen B.; Stevens, Richard; Shaw, Nancy L., comps. 2004. Restoring western ranges and wildlands. Gen. Tech. Rep. RMRS GTR-136. Fort Collins, CO: U.S. Department of Agriculture, Forest Service, Rocky Mountain Research Station. 3 volumes, 884 p.

This three-volume set provides background on philosophy, processes, plant materials selection, site preparation and seed and seeding equipment for revegetating disturbed rangelands, emphasizing use of native species. The conclusions and recommendations were drawn, in part, from research experiences on the Great Basin Experimental Range where the first efforts were begun that culminated in this publication.

114. Monsen, Stephen, B.; Stevens, Richard; Walker, Scott C. 1996. The competitive influence of seeded smooth brome (*Bromus inermis*) and intermediate wheatgrass (*Thinopyron intermedium*) within aspen-mountain brush communities of central Utah. In: West, N. E., ed. Rangelands in a sustainable biosphere, proceedings of the Fifth International Rangeland Congress; 1995 July 23-25; Salt Lake City, UT. Volume 1. Denver, CO: Society for Range Management: 379-380.

Ecological relationships of smooth brome (*Bromus inermis*) and intermediate wheatgrass (*Thinopyron intermedium*) with native species were investigated through comparison of seeded and nonseeded sites on the Great Basin Research Area (Great Basin Experimental Range), Manti-La Sal National Forest. Within a 40-year period, the two sod-forming seeded grasses gained dominance and reduced native herbs and shrubs. Both introduced grasses as commonly planted to stabilize wildlands, but are proving to be non-compatible with most native species and ultimately dominate seeded sites.

115. Nelson, Enoch W. 1930. Mapping of browse areas. Journal of Forestry 28(1): 91-92.

Since the meter quadrat method of charting cannot be used in mapping large browse specimens, the following methods have been devised for mapping browse sample plots at the Great Basin Experiment Station (Great Basin Experimental Range). The plots used vary in size from 1 to 3 square rods. Each browse specimen on a plot is accurately located on a map, which shows the location of the stem or stems of the plant as well as the crown spread. In mapping the browse specimens two methods may be used. One of these is the traverse board method. Several set-ups of the board are made over the plot that is being mapped, each set-up being directly over a permanent peg. A steel surveyor's tape is attached to the peg underneath the traverse board for obtaining distances to the various browse plants. The other method is the gridiron method. In it the plot is subdivided into small units with the aid of cord, surveyor's pins, and a steel measuring tape. Different points are located by measuring out from the intersection of the cord and then shown on a map sheet that has been ruled off into small units to correspond to the subdivisions of the plot. As a check against measurement of grazing use, plant vigor experiments were started in which the twigs and leaves of birchleaf mahogany (*Cercocarpus montanus*) and snowberry (*Symphoricarpos oreophilus*) are clipped to various intensities and at various times during the growing season. The ability to maintain the vigor of twig and leaves clipped under the different methods of treatment is noted.

116. Nelson, Enoch W. 1930. Methods of studying shrubby plants in relation to grazing. Ecology 11(4): 764-769.

During the past five years, methods for studying shrubby vegetation in range management and watershed protection investigations have been developed at the Great Basin Experimental Range near Ephraim, Utah. The methods are used to obtain detailed data in the field on the character and extent of shrub cover, plant succession in the brush type, rate and period of growth of shrub species, and the influence of grazing and other factors on these plants. The methods involve (1) mapping shrubby plants by species on selected areas; (2) recording stages of development and measuring growth throughout the growing season; (3) observing and measuring growth throughout the grazing season, and (4) clipping shrubs to determine empirically the influence of various intensities of grazing upon their yield and vigor. The controlled clipping studies were supplemented by hurdle plots to be opened and closed to grazing at certain intervals during the grazing season. It is expected that the data developed by these methods may indicate the value of various shrub species for grazing, and will be of value as a basis for developing adequate range management and watershed conservation of brush lands.

117. Norman, Liane Ellison. 2012. Breathing the West: Great Basin poems. Huron, OH: Bottom Dog Press. 94 p.

These poems are drawn, in part, from the journals of the author's father, Great Basin Station (Great Basin Experimental Range) Director and eminent ecologist Lincoln Ellison as well as her memories of the natural world and growing up, in part, at the Great Basin Station. Of the 70 poems included in this book, 14 treat life at the Station and another 11 are descriptive, philosophical, or insightful of ecology and natural history drawn from her father's journal entries or her experiences at the Station.

118. Norman, Liane Ellison. 2012. Roundtrip. Pittsburgh, PA: Yesterday's Party Press. 38 p.

This booklet of 26 poems of the author's insights of life includes 16 poems that are also presented in the previous entry. Eight of them deal with life growing up at the Great Basin Station (Great Basin Experimental Range) or with ecology and natural history there.

119. Orr, Howard K. 1957. Effects of plowing and seeding on some forage production and hydrologic characteristics of a subalpine range on central Utah. Res. Pap. INT-47. Ogden, UT: U.S. Department of Agriculture, Forest Service, Intermountain Forest and Range Experiment Station. 23 p.

Reseeding and protection from grazing for 3 years brought about a substantial improvement in the quality and quantity of subalpine-herbaceous forage on parts of the Manti Canyon range rehabilitation project area. By the third year of the improvement program, the tested portion of the treated area also provided control of surface runoff, infiltration, and erosion approximately equal to that of untreated, paired areas. Further improvement in both forage production and control of storm runoff and erosion should occur in the next few years providing the treated area is so managed as to allow for the full development of the newly established young plants, for the establishment and growth of new seedlings, and for the accumulation of litter. Additional measurements will be required in the years ahead to determine the potential effects of the treatment program. The Great Basin Experimental Range was integral to this study.

120. Parker, Kenneth, W.; Blaisdell, James P. 1968. Renovating big-game ranges. In: USDA Yearbook of Agriculture, Science for better living. Washington, DC: Government Printing Office: 223-229.

Those old "happy hunting grounds" of the great army of American sportsmen are being restored in the West. In years past, domestic livestock or big-game animals or both have seriously over used vast areas. The plants, which provided the best forage, have been destroyed in the process. This problem is especially acute during severe winters with deep snow when the herds of deer and elk cannot find enough food, and so many animals starve to death. Fortunately, this problem is being vigorously attacked, and much progress has already been made from Arizona to Montana and from California to the Dakotas. A man with a "green thumb," A. Perry Plummer, a dedicated Forest Service scientist in charge of the Great Basin Experimental Range, is one of several who are uncovering the know-how for successfully restoring valuable food and cover plants, both for domestic and wild animals. His work is on Intermountain rangelands. Thousands of acres of big-game winter range have already been improved. But much remains to be done, both by researchers and land administrators. Millions of acres in the West need renovation. Of course, there is a large backlog of information on seeding on ranges with grasses, developed by research since the turn of the century by the State agricultural experiment stations and the U.S. Department of Agriculture. But, this article is mainly the story of restoration of ranges with shrubs, often referred to as "browse," on which comparatively little research has been done. The research effort led by Plummer has been aimed mainly at finding desirable grasses, forbs, and shrubs suitable for restoring deteriorated winter ranges; determining planting requirements for individual species; and developing methods for seeding and planting, including elimination of the competition caused by unwanted vegetation.

121. Pearce, C. Kenneth; Hull, A. C., Jr. 1943. Some economic aspects of reseeding range lands. Journal of Forestry 41(5): 346-358.

Successful plantings of deteriorated rangelands have attracted much attention throughout the Intermountain region in recent years. Well-planned and carefully executed reseeding projects produce good stands that significantly improve the range. The cost-benefit relationships of this work, however, need to be more critically examined. The need for increased meat and wool production in our war effort and the promise of range reseeding as a huge work reservoir in post-war conservation program makes the consideration of the subject particularly timely. Activities on the Great Basin Experimental Range were integral to the conclusions drawn in this report.

122. Pearce, C. Kenneth; Plummer, A. Perry; Savage, D. A. 1948. Restoring the range by reseeding. In: USDA Yearbook of Agriculture. Washington, DC: Government Printing Office: 227-233.

Full restoration of much of the rangeland in need of improvement will require more than better grazing management. About 80 million acres of rangeland have been so badly depleted that they will have to be reseeded artificially if they are to recover in our generation. Satisfactory methods have not yet been developed for reseeding all situations, but progress is being made. Already more than 5 million acres have been planted. Range reseeding is usually done on an extensive basis on lands unsuited for cultivation and at comparatively low cost. Plowing, except to reduce competition from undesirable plants, is usually not attempted; seedbeds are not generally prepared. Reseeding, to be most effective, should be done where the chance of success is good and where increased forage will help most in making better use of the land and in increasing livestock production. For each area to be seeded, success depends on knowing what to seed, when to seed, and how to seed economically. Activities on the Great Basin Experimental Range were integral to the conclusions drawn in this report.

123. Pechanec, Joseph F. 1940. Forest Service range research seminar. Ecology 21(3): 422-424.

During the period July 10 to 22, 1939, a seminar on range research methods and procedures was held by the Forest Service, United States Department of Agriculture, at the Great Basin Experiment Station near Ephraim, Utah, a branch of the Intermountain Forest and Range Experiment Station, with headquarters at Ogden, Utah. Washington Office representatives of the divisions of range research, range management, and wildlife management, the directors, division leaders, and range research staff members of the western regional forest and range experiment stations, the assistant regional foresters in charge of wildlife and range management of the western forest regions, and several other Forest Service members were in attendance. This was the second meeting of this type to be held at the Great Basin Station during the last 10-year period. In 1931, an ecological and range methodology meeting was held under the auspices of the Ecological Society of America. Ecologists throughout the West participated. The purpose of the 1939 intra-bureau meeting was to aid in strengthening the Forest Service attack on the broad western range problems and to redefine or clarify the objectives of the range research organization. Discussion centered on the problems being encountered, the methods to be used in their solution, and the other measures necessary to facilitate the conduct of range research and the dissemination of results. At the time of the 1939 meeting, range research had to its credit such contributions as the development of rotation deferred system of grazing, invention and development of range reconnaissance or range surveys, foundation data on growth requirements and value of range plants, improved methods for grazing sheep and goats such as open and quiet herding and bedding them down in a new place every night, improved salting and better-placed watering places, the eradication of tall larkspur, the building of indicators of range conditions, and the crusading against range deterioration and erosion. These are contributions to management of the western ranges. But ahead are many complex problems such as the determination of the grazing capacity of western range types, proper degree and season of use for many of the key forage species, standards of range forage utilization, methods of artificial range revegetation, and improved methods of securing livestock distribution on the range. Inadequate information on these and closely related problems such as the correction of nutritional deficiencies of range livestock, plant breeding as an approach to forage improvement, interrelationships of rodents and other wildlife with range livestock, and the social and economic aspects of range livestock management hindering the most efficient use of range forage resources.

124. Plummer, A. Perry. 1946. Mountain bromegrass—good for seeding mountain ranges. National Wool Grower 36(5): 14.

Native mountain bromegrass (*Bromus carinatus*) is an excellent grass for seeding mountain ranges in the Intermountain region that receive in excess of 14 inches of annual precipitation. It is strictly a bunchgrass but establishes itself readily, is aggressive, matures quickly, and is productive. This grass species is particularly well adapted for seeding under aspen depleted of the herbaceous undercover. Merely broadcasting the seed under aspen just prior to, during, or immediately after leaf fall has produced good stands. Mountain brome is one of the most aggressive grasses in establishing itself on annual weed openings and on raw depleted soils. Brush flats

USDA Forest Service Gen. Tech. Rep. RMRS-GTR-305WWW. 2013

62

on the higher mountains can also be successfully sown to mountain bromegrass. On areas that are occupied with other vegetation, however, whether annual weeds or brush, it pays to eliminate such vegetation prior to seeding. Experience on the Great Basin Experimental Range was integral to this report.

125. Plummer, A. Perry. 1947. Make Utah ranges productive…artificial seeding of rangelands will help protect the livestock industry of our State. Utah Farmer 67(1): 26; 67(2): 10, 23.

Past plantings show that from two to many times more forage can be grown on many Utah ranges when seeded by proper methods to adapted species. For example, yields from 12 early test plantings established from 17 to 35 years ago at the Great Basin Research Center (Great Basin Experimental Range) in Ephraim Canyon are currently producing increased forage yields equivalent to more than one cow month or five sheep months pasturage an acre more than the adjacent nonseeded range. The plantings are on mountain brush, aspen, and high mountain meadows.

126. Plummer, A. Perry. 1959. Restoration of juniper-pinyon ranges in Utah. Proceedings, Society of American Foresters 1958: 207-211.

In 1956 and 1957, 10 and 11 years after the seeding, current production was estimated on small plots enclosing old sagebrush and rabbitbrush plants and on similar plots away from the shrubs. Estimated grass yields were virtually the same whether brush was present or absent; this suggests that the shrubs were not suppressing grass production appreciably. If so, the browse produced by 790 plants per acre of big sagebrush and 990 of rubber rabbitbrush may be considered as a bonus in ground cover and in browse for game and sheep. A similar apparent lack of suppression of grass by shrubs has been noted in the mountain brush zone where old plantings of grass were growing with several shrub species. These observations are contrary to many others on grass-shrub associations, but they may be valid under certain conditions. They point to the need for a better evaluation of the part shrubs may play in making ranges most productive. Certainly there is a balance of browse and herbaceous cover that is more productive than either class alone. Experience on the Great Basin Experimental Range was integral to this report.

127. Plummer, A. Perry. 1960. Restoring mule deer range. In: Bond, Jim. The mule deer. Portland, OR: Conger Printing Company: 109-112.

The information in this book chapter included in author Jim Bond's book was drawn, in part, from the author's experiences at the Great Basin Experimental Range. Utah and the Great Basin is a land of shrubs. Mule deer are well adapted to shrub habitats. However there has been a substantial attrition of important mule deer forage and cover plants including antelope bitterbrush, curl-leaf mahogany, fourwing saltbush, and winterfat as well as elimination on many winter ranges of the early spring-growing broadleaf herbs and grasses that produce succulent and high protein forage needed to sustain winter-weakened does and their offspring. It is necessary to reverse this attrition through habitat restoration if healthy deer populations are to be sustained. The most important part of restoring game ranges is to have seed available of well-adapted plants. Among important qualifications of suitable plants are that they have enough amplitude of adaptation and establishment to be useful over a wide range of sites. To discover the amplitude of adaptation as rapidly as possible, species and populations are first planted in small plots on an area relatively near the lower and upper edges of the deer winter range. Establishment of desirable species can be accomplished by transplanting or by seeding. These techniques are being evaluated for effectiveness.

128. Plummer, A. Perry. 1967. Experimental crownvetch plantings. Range Improvement Notes. U.S. Department of Agriculture, Forest Service, Intermountain Region 12(2): 13-14.

In Ephraim Canyon on the Great Basin Experimental Range on the Manti-LaSal National Forest, experimental plantings of crownvetch (*Coronilla varia*) during the past 4 years have been observed. Crownvetch is native to the Mediterranean basin. The plantings have been evaluated for adaptability and erosion control and for possible usefulness as game forage. They were planted in openings in the oakbrush zone at an elevation of 7,100 feet with an average annual precipitation of about 16 inches. Both direct seeding and seedling transplants from greenhouse grown plants were established and evaluated. The seed was inoculated with the nodule bacteria (*Rhizobia*). Overall performance by both direct seeding and transplants has been outstanding.

129. Plummer, A. Perry. 1970. Plants for revegetation of roadcuts and other disturbed or eroded areas. Range Improvement Notes, U.S. Department of Agriculture, Forest Service, Intermountain Region 15(1): 1-8.

A fairly large number of shrub and herb species can be used to cover and stabilize eroded areas such as roadcuts, fills, roadsides and seriously eroded areas. The areas treated in this research were those from which the topsoil had been largely removed. Six major purposes for establishing vegetation on such areas are: (1) Stabilize the site against erosion and reduce hazards of silt pollution in streams; (2) prevent undesirable plants from gaining a competitive foothold; (3) beautify the area with desirable vegetation; (4) establish vegetation to screen unsightly backgrounds; (5) furnish shade and food for wildlife; (6) provide shade and pleasant environment for people. Nursery stock, greenhouse and cold frame seedlings, cuttings, and wildings were used in transplanting experiments. Direct seeding was used as well, especially for herbaceous species. In this review, emphasis was placed on shrubs because of the recent demand for such information. The merits of more than 90 shrub species as well as about two dozen species of forbs and grasses are given. In carrying out revegetation plantings, special attention should be given to the following principles: (1) use only species and ecotypes adapted to the site; (2) plant mixtures, rather than single species, that will stabilize the soil and harmonize with the landscape; (3) make certain that transplants are properly planted and that seeds are adequately covered; (4) do planting in a suitable season; (5) reduce competition from other vegetation to adequate levels; (6) protect planted areas from damage by animals. Experience on the Great Basin Experimental Range was integral to this report.

USDA Forest Service Gen. Tech. Rep. RMRS-GTR-305WWW. 2013

64

130. Plummer, A. Perry. 1974. Oldman wormwood to stabilize disturbed areas. Utah Science 35(March): 26-27.

Oldman wormwood (*Artemisia abrotanum*), sometimes called southern wood, European sage, and ornamental sage, is a European shrub that was successfully introduced into the United States during the 19th century. Over the past 35 years it has proved well adapted to the wide variety of soils that range from fairly alkaline and fairly acidic in the Intermountain West including the Great Basin Experimental Range and other parts of the Wasatch Plateau and Wasatch Mountains. It is established best from rooted cuttings.

131. Plummer, A. Perry. 1976. Shrubs for the subalpine zone of the Wasatch Plateau. In: Zuck, R. H.; Brown, L. F., eds. Proceedings: High altitude revegetation workshop No. 2. Fort Collins, CO: Colorado State University Information Series No. 21: 33-40.

Most of the native shrubs on the subalpine areas of the Great Basin Experimental Range on the Wasatch Plateau have been trial planted. Wildlings of some species were transplanted as early as 1913. These early trials, and more recent direct seeding and transplanting experiments, have identified a number of shrubs that have promise as ground cover and forage. Important among these are mountain snowberry (*Symphoricarpos oreophilus*), lanceleaf rabbitbrush (*Chrysothamnus viscidiflorus* ssp. *lanceolatus*), Rothrock big sagebrush (*Artemisia tridentata* ssp. *rothrockii*), redberry elder (*Sambucus racemosa* ssp. *pubescens var. microbotrys*), and mountain big sagebrush (*Artemisia tridentata* ssp. *vaseyana*). Mechanical seed harvesting appears feasible for some shrubs, but, to a large extent, hand techniques are necessary. The development of seed orchards at lower elevations appears feasible.

132. Plummer, A. Perry. 1977. Revegetation of disturbed Intermountain Area sites. In: Thames, John L., ed. Reclamation and use of disturbed Intermountain sites. Tucson, AZ: University of Arizona Press: 302-339.

A number of shrubs, grasses, trees, and forbs are useful for revegetating bare or eroded areas by direct seeding or transplanting. While there are new species and variants to be discovered or developed for particular sites, and sufficient numbers of adapted plants are known for fairly adequate revegetation of most sites, seeds and transplanting stock may not be available for some species. A critical need exists for areas from which desirable and adapted plants can be readily obtained for transplanting. To get the needed plant materials assembled requires planning 2 to 5 years ahead. Unfortunately, this is generally not done. The species adaptation attributes and adaptation of disturbance areas for some 130 shrub and tree species, 40 forb species, and 35 grass species were evaluated for use in revegetation projects. The beginning background research and some continuing research for revegetation was conducted at the Great Basin Experimental Range.

133. Plummer, A. Perry; Christensen, Donald R; Monsen, Stephen B. 1967. Highlights, results and accomplishments of game range restoration studies, 1966. Restoring big game ranges in Utah. Publication No. 67-4. Salt Lake City, UT: Utah Division of Fish and Game. 45 p.

This publication, based in part on results from the Great Basin Experimental Range, relates accomplishments and highlights of findings from the past year's investigative endeavor. An attempt has been made to integrate the most current results with those of the former 10 years. Results are derived from activities under 17 objectives divided among 7 jobs: (1) species adaptation, (2) recognition of suitable sites, (3) germination, (4) site preparation and planting, (5) protecting plantings from biological factors, (6) species and cover changes on restored areas, and (7) formulation of practical recommendations. By way of detail, there are more than 100 species, including shrubs, forbs, and grasses, which have shown sufficient adaptation to establish them as useful in improving habitat in some important way for game.

134. Plummer, A. Perry; Christensen, Donald R; Monsen, Stephen B. 1968. Restoring big game ranges in Utah. Publication No. 68-3. Salt Lake City, UT: Utah Division of Fish and Game. 183 p.

Artificial restoration of Utah's extensive, but often depleted, big game ranges can greatly increase productivity for both game and livestock, and can also improve soil stability. All important ranges of the state support upland game, and runoff from these areas drains into streams and lakes that support aquatic life on which fish and waterfowl subsist. Consequently, restoration of low-producing, eroding game range areas is urgently required. This bulletin reports what has been learned about adapted plants and useful techniques for improving range productivity beginning with work on the Great Basin Experimental Range. It also describes procedures and treatments that have proved to be effective. Much of the big game range in states adjacent to Utah is plagued by the same problems that beset Utah range; hence the treatments reported here will be useful in improving extensive range areas in these neighboring states.

135. Plummer, A. Perry; Christensen, Donald R.; Stevens, Richard; Hancock, Norman V. 1970. Improvement of forage for habitat and game. In: 50th annual conference of Western Association of State Game and Fish Commissioners; 1970 15 July: 1-12.

Ten principles for successful restoration of Utah game ranges are given: (1) Changes in plant cover by the proposed measures must be determined to be desirable—often a change in management to permit lighter grazing by livestock so that desirable species can develop may be all that is required. (2) Terrain and soil types must be suited to changes selected—the soil and terrain should be carefully considered to determine where appropriate treatment would produce the most forage for game. (3) Precipitation must be adequate to assure establishment and survival of seeded plants—the amount of precipitation, along with occurrence of indicator plants, is

USDA Forest Service Gen. Tech. Rep. RMRS-GTR-305WWW. 2013

66

the most important guide to what species may be seeded successfully. (4) Competition must be low enough to assure that desired species can be established—anchor chaining has been developed as a highly versatile, effective, economical, and widely applicable method for eliminating competition of trees and shrubs. (5) Only species and strains of plants adapted to the area should be planted—seeded species must be able to establish and maintain themselves and there should be a balance of shrubs, forbs, and grasses. (6) Mixtures, rather than single species, should be planted—it is advantageous to seed mixtures when the major purpose of restoration is for the improvement of game range. (7) Sufficient seed of acceptable purity and viability should be planted to assure getting a stand—the amount per acre depends on seed purity, size and viability, and whether seeds are drilled or broadcast. (8) Seed must be covered sufficiently—deeper than ½ inch planting is seldom desirable and leaving seed exposed is unsatisfactory. (9) Planting should be done in the season of optimum conditions for establishment—whenever climate permits, seeding in the winter is best. (10) The planted area must be adequately protected—young plants and seedlings should not be grazed or severely trampled by livestock, big game, rabbits, rodents, or insects. Experience on the Great Basin Experimental Range was integral to this report.

136. Plummer, A. Perry; Fenley, John M. 1950. Seasonal periods for planting grasses in the subalpine zone of central Utah. Research Paper 18. Ogden, UT: U.S. Department of Agriculture, Forest Service, Intermountain Forest and Range Experiment Station. 12 p.

Comparison of seasonal planting for grasses useful for revegetation in the subalpine zone of the Great Basin Experimental Range showed that winterkill is responsible for the high seedling mortality from planting in the later summer and early fall.

137. Plummer, A. Perry; Frischknecht, Neil C. 1952. Increasing field stands of Indian ricegrass. Agronomy Journal 44(6): 285-289.

Spring and fall planting trials using three intensities of acid treatment on 10 lots of seed were conducted at three different field locations (dry desert shadscale, valley sagebrush, and mountain brush) in which Indian ricegrass had been a prominent component of the indigenous vegetation. Under field conditions the two lighter acid treatments, which only weakened the seed coat, gave higher emergence. The degree of treatment can be determined by inspection; it should be enough to soften the seed coat thoroughly but not enough to expose the endosperm. It is probably that the ultimate solution to the problem of obtaining successful stands of Indian ricegrass will be the selection of strains adaptable to differing soil and climatic conditions. In the meantime, locally grown seed, acid-treated to not exceed a moderate intensity, will improve field stands. Study sites from the Great Basin Experimental Range were used in this report.

138. Plummer, A. Perry; Hull, A. C., Jr.; Stewart, George; Robertson, Joseph H. 1955. Seeding rangelands in Utah, Nevada, southern Idaho, and western Wyoming. Agric. Handb. No. 71. Washington, DC: U.S. Department of Agriculture, Forest Service. 73 p.

Artificial seeding of immense areas of deteriorated rangeland in the Intermountain region (Utah, Nevada, southern Idaho, and western Wyoming) now offers a major and direct means of vastly increasing forage production and controlling erosion. This is possible because of up-to-date information developed by more than 20 years of experimental planting. In this period nearly 1,000 species and species variants from all parts of the globe have been tested. Trials with these have been conducted on the most important problem areas by many field methods. It is conservatively estimated that a total area of approximately 20 million acres of deteriorated rangeland in the Intermountain region should be revegetated, either for forage production or for watershed protection and soil stabilization. Increased forage production on this seedable area will help to obtain the lighter use necessary for improving an additional 100 million acres of damaged range, which can be rehabilitated more economically through proper management. Advantages from successfully seeded ranges are immediate and direct to livestock operators. Experience on the Great Basin Experimental Range was integral to this report.

139. Plummer, A. Perry, Hurd, Richard M.; Pearse, C. K. 1943. How to reseed Utah range lands. Res. Pap. 1. Ogden, Utah: U.S. Department of Agriculture, Forest Service, Intermountain Forest and Range Experiment Station. 22 p.

Artificial reseeding can increase the forage production on many acres of Utah rangelands. Careful planting by proper yet inexpensive methods will produce good stands on many valley and foothill lands now covered with annual weeds, cheatgrass, saltgrass, or brush, and on mountain lands in the mountain brush, aspen, and subalpine zones. Important principles for determining where reseeding should be done, what species and methods should be used, and how the reseeded stand should be grazed to keep it productive, have been developed from recent research studies. Experience on the Great Basin Experimental Range was integral to this report.

140. Plummer, A. Perry; Jensen, Robert L. 1956. Job completion report for artificial revegetation studies on big-game ranges in Utah, W-82-R-1, A Pittman-Robertson Project, March 1, 1955 – March 1, 1956. Salt Lake City, UT: Utah Department of Fish and Game. 28 p.

Slightly more than one year has elapsed since the game forage project was organized in Utah under a cooperative agreement between the Utah State Department of Fish and Game and the Intermountain Forest and Range Experiment Station of the U.S. Department of Agriculture, Forest Service. Nearly all effort has been on winter ranges. Great emphasis has been placed here because the wellbeing of the State's greatest wildlife resource rests on this habitat or meeting place of mountain and lowland, characterized by pigmy forest, brush, and open ground. It is also characterized by great diversity of slope and soil. Great emphasis has been placed on finding adapted plants. To do so, 30 to 36 species consisting of nursery stock, wildings (native root cuttings and transplants), and stem cuttings were established in three test sites including one on the Great Basin Experimental Range.

141. Plummer, A. Perry; Jensen, Robert L.; Stapley, Homer. 1957. Job completion report for game forage revegetation project, W-82-R-2, A Pittman-Robertson Project, March 1, 1956 – February 28, 1957. Salt Lake City, UT: Utah Department of Fish and Game. 128 p.

This ongoing research project, drawing in part from activities in the Great Basin Experimental Range, has as its objectives (1) determination of the desirable species of forage, native and introduced that can be grown on various sites with emphasis on species that have shown promise through previous research; (2) determination of how to recognize sites to which various species are adapted; (3) determination of conditions that are favorable to germination of seeds and to establishment by vegetative propagation; (4) determination of methods of preparing sites for planting; (5) determination of suitable planting and propagation techniques; (6) determination of methods of protecting seeds and seedlings from rodent, bird, and insect depredations, and from other adverse environmental factors; and (7) formulation of practical recommendations for restoring game forage species on these ranges. Experience on the Great Basin Experimental Range was integral to this report.

142. Plummer, A. Perry; Jensen, Robert L.; Stapley, Homer. 1957. Range revegetation. Utah Fish and Game Magazine 13(6): 8-9.

Utah, particularly, its browse ranges, offers fascinating areas for discovering the plants to fill important requirements for range revegetation. Testing sites around the state and research on the Great Basin Experimental Range are providing valuable insights. Utah includes a wide diversity of site conditions, from the standpoint of competition, soil, erosion, and elevation to provide establishment opportunities for revegetation plant materials from nature and from selection practices. The plant materials available include exotic species that are being tested for adaptation as well as many native plant species. There is good prospect that investigation of natives will give new insight and a better approach to forage improvement that will lead to better sustained production on wildlands.

143. Plummer, A. Perry; Jensen, Robert L.; Stapley, Homer. 1958. Job completion report for game forage revegetation project, W-82-R-3, A Pittman-Robertson Project, March 1, 1957 – February, 1958. Salt Lake City, UT: Utah Department of Fish and Game. 175 p.

Emphasis in this report is on winter deer range and has drawn information and results, in part, from the Great Basin Experimental Range. Concentration has been on the juniper-pinyon belt, a type that covers more than one-fourth of the state and is a vital component of the winter range for big game. Primary concern is with adaptation of suitable shrubs for planting these areas, although increasing time is being devoted to other phases, and particularly to methods of planting and effects of juniper-pinyon tree removal on improvement of natural and seeded understory. Removal or thinning of this overstory of pigmy forest appears to usually be an essential aspect to improvement of the understory cover where it is depleted and severely suppressed. Several new shrubs have been included in transplant trials with nursery stock or wildings. Of these, black sagebrush looks promising, particularly for establishment on severe sites. Tatarian honeysuckle appears the most outstanding in adaptation over a period of three years to the broad variation in sites. Close rivals are Russian olive, Siberian peashrub, western sandcherry, and big sagebrush.

144. Plummer, A. Perry; Jorgensen, Kent R. 1978. Harvesting, cleaning, and storing seed of western shrubs. In: Conference & workshop proceedings; 1978 October, Western Forest Nursery Council and Intermountain Nurseryman's Combined Nurseyman's conference and seed processing workshop, Eureka, CA: D-65-D-75.

This review briefly relates what is being done to harvest and clean shrub seeds to make them available for wildland areas, and to point out some of the future needs for this class of plants. Cleaning and storing are important parts of handling the seeds and making them available. Compared with harvesting and cleaning and getting seeds ready to plant, storage is less demanding but is still a pertinent aspect and must be done properly to keep good seeds available. Experience on the Great Basin Experimental Range was integral to this report.

145. Plummer, A. Perry; Stapley, Homer D. 1960. Research on game forage restoration in Utah. In: Proceedings of the Thirty-ninth annual conference of Western Association of State Game and Fish Commissioners; 1959 June 29-30, July 1; Portland, OR.

Need for improvement of many Utah game ranges has long been recognized. Since this project was begun, it has been determined that numerous problems can be solved in the near term. Pilot plantings have yielded information that will help in designing and implementing larger plantings. Recent conclusions from pilot plantings give great encouragement about what can be accomplished by revegetation on Utah game ranges. To develop the groundwork, it will require earnest research. The nature of this investigation requires intensive hard work and the courage to experiment freely. The project is organized in six phases with objectives of determining (1) adapted plant species; (2) suitable planting sites; (3) conditions favorable to germination; (4) effective methods of planting and propagation; (5) ways of protecting seeds and young plants for animal predation; and (6) practical procedures for restoring game ranges. Experience on the Great Basin Experimental Range was integral to this report.

146. Plummer, A. Perry; Stapley, Homer D.; Christensen, Donald R. 1959. Job completion report for game forage revegetation project, W-82-R-4, A Pittman-Robertson Project, March 1, 1958 – February 28, 1959. Salt Lake City, UT: Utah Department of Fish and Game. 25 p.

In this first 4 years of the project, attention has been concentrated on fall, winter, and spring ranges (referred to hereafter as winter ranges), all of which cover essentially the same land. While game habitat on summer ranges also needs improvement, the problems on these higher ranges are small in comparison to those of restoring the winter ranges where big game in Utah must live more than 6 months out of each year. Action on restoration of summer ranges must be held in abeyance until major problems for the winter ranges are solved. Experience on the Great Basin Experimental Range was integral to this report.

147. Plummer, A. Perry; Stewart, George. 1944. Seeding grass on deteriorated aspen range. Res. Pap. 11. Ogden, UT: U.S. Department of Agriculture, Forest Service, Intermountain Forest and Range Experiment Station. 6 p.

The herbaceous undercover on much of the aspen range in the Intermountain region is badly deteriorated. These naturally highly productive areas, when revegetated, can contribute greatly towards a much-needed supply of range forage. One of the major obstacles to successful seeding has been the difficulty of getting the seeds covered with soil since both standing and fallen trees interfere with the use of drills, harrows, or other machinery. In the search for methods to overcome this difficulty, it was found that for open aspen stands the covering of seeds is unnecessary when the right precautions are taken in other phases of planting. When seeds are broadcast shortly before, during, or soon after leaf fall, the leaves form a mat that conserves the surface soil moisture long enough for young seedlings to establish. Fourteen species (bearded wheatgrass, mountain bromegrass, blue wildrye, tall oatgrass, orchardgrass, slender wheatgrass, mountain lupine, smooth bromegrass, Letterman needlegrass, showy goldeneye, Canada wildrye, meadow fescue, big bluegrass, and Kentucky bluegrass) were broadcast on four plots, 10 x 14 feet, prior to leaf fall and immediately after leaf fall in 1941 and 1942 in the Great Basin Experimental Range, Manti National Forest. The results of this ongoing study tentatively indicate that seeding under aspen without covering the seeds is an effective means of establishing understory species.

148. Prevedel, David A.; McArthur, E. Durant; Johnson, Curtis M. 2005. Beginnings of range management: an anthology of the Sampson-Ellison photo plots (1913-2003) and a short history of the Great Basin Experiment Station. Gen. Tech. Rep. RMRS-GTR-154. Fort Collins, CO: U.S. Department of Agriculture, Forest Service, Rocky Mountain Research Station. 60 p.

High-elevation watersheds on the Wasatch Plateau in central Utah were severely overgrazed in the late 1800s, resulting in catastrophic flooding and mudflows through adjacent communities. Affected citizens petitioned the Federal government to establish a Forest Reserve (1902), and the Transfer Act of 1905 established the Manti National Forest. The Great Basin Station (Great Basin Experimental Range), a forerunner of the Intermountain Forest and Range Experiment Station, was created in 1911 within this area to study the influence of rangeland vegetation on erosion and floods. This publication contains a collection of 12 recurring sets of photographs that started in 1913 on these depleted high-elevation rangelands. The sites were re-photographed in the 1940s, 1972, 1990, and 2003. It is also a tribute to two men who pioneered the science of range management—Arthur W. Sampson and Lincoln Ellison. As Directors of the Experiment Station, they initiated and maintained the early photo sites and study plots. It was with these photograph records and study plots that many of the interpretations and guidelines for the management of high-elevation watersheds were developed. After 90 years, plant community changes on these high-elevation watersheds have led to a vegetation composition significantly different than the original condition. New plant communities have reached thresholds where yearly vegetative composition appears to be climate driven. Many of the higher elevation areas remain in unsatisfactory watershed health with active erosion.

149. Price, Raymond. 1938. Artificial reseeding on oak-brush range in central Utah. Circular 458. Washington, DC: U.S. Department of Agriculture.19 p.

Artificial reseeding trials were conducted by the Great Basin Branch of the Intermountain Forest and Range Experiment Station (Great Basin Experimental Range) at three different elevational experimental areas on a typical oak-brush range in central Utah. The experimental plots were sown during the period 1928 to 1931 and the last observations reported were made in the fall of 1935. Crested wheatgrass (*Agropyron cristatum*), smooth brome (*Bromus inermis*), and mountain brome (*B. carinatus*) produced good stands at the lower, middle, and upper experimental areas of the oak-brush range. Crested wheatgrass plants were more vigorous at the two lower areas and smooth brome and mountain brome plants increased in vigor with increases in elevation. Slender wheatgrass (*Agropyron pauciflorum*) produced good stands at the middle area, the only place it was sown. White sweetclover (*Melilotus alba*,) and yellow sweetclover (*M. officinalis*) produced poor to no stands at all areas, although both species maintained some plants in swales or low areas where soil and moisture conditions were above average. The best stands on all plantings were obtained by broadcasting seed on plowed furrows, spaced approximately 3 feet apart and covering by use of a brush drag, at a cost of $6 per acre exclusive of the cost of the seed. Some fair to good stands of grasses were obtained by broadcasting seed on unprepared ground and by broadcasting seed on unprepared ground followed by trampling by sheep, at costs of 65 cents and 80 cents per acre, respectively, exclusive of the cost of the seed. A few tests were made by broadcasting seed on plowed furrows with no further treatment, at a cost of $4.50 per acre, exclusive of cost of seed, and by broadcasting seed on snow. During a period of 7 years the grazing capacity of plots reseeded to grasses by sowing seed on plowed furrows and covering by use of a brush drag, in a heavy sagebrush cover type at the lower experimental area, was increased over that of the open grazed unseeded plots from 367 to 933 percent, depending upon the species sown. Similar data showed increases of from 71 to 129 percent in an oak brush-sagebrush cover type at the upper area. Increases of 57 percent were noted at the middle area from plots reseeded to grasses by broadcasting and trampling by sheep. Some of the increase was due to increase of the native vegetation resulting in part from restricted livestock grazing and in part from cultivation accompanying the sowing treatments. Practically equally good stands were obtained from both spring and fall sowings when precipitation following planting was normal or above. However, fall sowings are recommended for similar oak-brush areas, since precipitation is more likely to be assured during early spring when the seedlings are becoming established.

Some degree of soil preparation followed by some means of covering the seed is necessary if successful reseeding is to be assured on sites where soil conditions are average or below in depth and texture on similar oak-brush ranges is indicated by the success of the species sown on plowed furrows and covered. The justification of the expense involved in artificial reseeding operations for extensive range use is dependent on the demand for the restoration of a vegetational cover, the degree of soil depletion, the extent of depletion of the native plant cover, and the facilities available. Additional research in reseeding is necessary (1) to determine the species ecologically adapted to specific range soil types; (2) to determine the possibilities of developing new strains by plant breeding; and (3) to develop practicable methods for extensive range application.

150. Price, Raymond; Evans, Robert B. 1937. Climate of the west front of the Wasatch Plateau in central Utah. Monthly Weather Review. 65(8): 291-301.

Climatic data presented in this study were collected during the 20-year period, 1914-1934, within the four main vegetational zones, designated as piñon-juniper, oakbrush, aspen-fir, and spruce-fir, ranging in elevation from 5,575 feet to 10,100 feet, in the Great Basin Experimental Range on the west front of the Wasatch Plateau in central Utah. Observations were made with standard meteorological equipment. Data collected and summarized include precipitation and atmospheric temperatures in the four vegetation zones. Precipitation and atmospheric temperatures of the area vary widely between vegetation zones, owing to differences of elevation and topography. Total annual precipitation varies from 11.70 inches in the piñon-juniper zone near the valley floor, to 29.48 inches in the aspen-fir zone near the middle of the plateau front, and 28.01 inches in the spruce-fir zone at the summit. Of these totals, 45 percent, 70 percent, and 80 percent of precipitation, respectively, is received during the winter season, November 1 to May 1, in the form of snow. Summer thunderstorms are interspersed with rainless periods that occur during the main growing season and have extended for 158 days, and longer, between occurrences of 0.50 inch or more precipitation. The trend of precipitation for the 34-year period, 1901 to 1934, inclusive, at the piñon-juniper zone shows considerable periodic variation characterized by above- and below-normal precipitation. Temperatures as high as 101°F. have been recorded in the piñon-juniper zone and as low as −30 °F in the oak-brush and aspen-fir zones. The growing season within the area is extremely short, the frost-free period being only 90 days in the oakbrush, 87 days in the aspen-fir, and 80 days in the spruce-fir zones.

151. Reynolds, Robert V. R. 1911. Grazing and floods: a study of conditions in the Manti National Forest, Utah. Bulletin 91. Washington, DC: U.S. Department of Agriculture, Forest Service. 16 p.

This report is responsible in part for the establishment of what eventually became the Great Basin Experimental Range. Heavy precipitation, steep slopes, and a comparatively scanty forest cover all tend to favor the occurrence of floods in the streams flowing from the Manti National Forest. This tendency was formerly counteracted to a great extent by an abundant ground cover of shrubs and grasses,

USDA Forest Service Gen. Tech. Rep. RMRS-GTR-305WWW. 2013

73

which delayed the run-off and prevented erosion. Previous to 1888 there is no record of serious floods in this region. Heavy grazing by horses, cattle, and especially by sheep resulted, however, in the almost complete destruction of this cover. Since 1888, floods of great violence and destructiveness have been common, and it is estimated that they have caused a total loss of approximately $225,000. Upon the creation of the Manti National Forest in 1903 prompt action was taken to prevent further damage to the range from overgrazing. Since 1903 no sheep have been allowed on the west side of the divide. Manti Canyon was still further protected by excluding all stock from an area of 8,830 acres on the uplands from 1904 to 1909. Since then a small number of drifting cattle and horses have been allowed on the area. As a result of this protection, range conditions within Manti Canyon have steadily improved, and at the same time it has been less subject to floods. A striking example of this was in August, 1909, when severe floods occurred in Ephraim and Six Mile Canyons, from which stock has never been completely excluded, while Manti Canyon, lying between them, escaped entirely. Also, on September 18 and 19, 1910, two successive floods caused damage of approximately $1,000 in Ephraim. No flood resulted at Manti, although the Manti watershed is nearly twice as great in extent as that which drains through Ephraim. At the request of members of the community, steps have now been taken to restrict grazing in the Forest still further. There can be no reasonable doubt that the torrents that have devastated this region within the last 20 years have been caused primarily by overgrazing, and that they can be largely controlled, if not entirely eliminated, by a restoration of the natural protective cover of shrubs and grasses.

152. Sampson, Arthur W. 1913. Scientific range management. National Wool Grower 3(12): 7-9.

Arthur Sampson

Salient points for restocking a depleted range: (1) Repeated removal of the forage in the spring of the year seriously weakens the plant. Premature grazing should be discontinued as a general practice. (2) Moderate grazing after seed maturity in no way interferes with the herbage production and seed crop and stirring of the soil through trampling is highly essential in securing reproduction. Grazing after seed maturity therefore should be practiced in the case of lands in need of reseeding. (3) The range should be grazed moderately after a seedling stand has been secured and no stock should be allowed on the land except late in the autumn until the young plants are firmly established. (4) The amount of range that may be set aside for autumn grazing will be determined by the time of seed maturity and amount of forage required for the stock to complete the season. (5) After the first area selected has been thoroughly reseeded it may be grazed relatively early in the season and another set aside for autumn grazing. This system of alternate grazing should be continued at all times in order to maintain the vigor of the vegetation. Observations and research on the Great Basin Experimental Range contributed to the conclusions presented in this report.

153. Sampson, Arthur W. 1914. Distribution and functions of range plants. National Wool Grower 4(12): 20-23.

For convenience in classifying grazing lands in a broad way, it is recommended that an "Ecological" classification of the range be considered in management that has to do with (1) the way plants are associated together in similar soils, and why some require one set of soil and moisture conditions and others quite different conditions; (2) the character and functions of the organs both below and above ground of vascular or higher plants such as grasses ; and (3) because of similarity in appearance of the leaves and habit of growth of grasses and grass-like plants but those two plant types can be distinguished from one another. Observations and research on the Great Basin Experimental Range contributed to the conclusions presented in this report.

154. Sampson, Arthur W. 1916. Bluegrasses with a discussion of chemical analysis. National Wool Grower (6): 23-25.

The group of bluegrasses known to botanists as *Poa*, belongs to the largest and most famous grass family or tribe that embraces the well-known fescues and bromes. All told there are as many as 140 different kinds of bluegrasses distributed throughout the world. In the United States there are about 75 different kinds. Three of these are annuals, but all the others are perennials. With but few exceptions the many native blue grasses, as well as those that have been domesticated, are palatable to all classes of stock during practically all seasons in the year. In many parts of the West they furnish more feed of the first quality than any other plant. In some localities, however, they occur rather sparsely, but are grazed with much relish. On the Manti National Forest, extensive grass reseeding experiments of Kentucky bluegrass has given unusually good results on the high summer pasturelands of the Great Basin Experimental Range at 10,000 feet in elevation.

155. Sampson, Arthur W. 1916. Artificial reseeding of range lands. National Wool Grower 6(11): 23-25.

The success or failure of artificial seeding (as opposed to the seeding of native species) is chiefly determined by (1) the kinds of plants seeded; (2) the time in the season that seed is scattered; (3) the thoroughness with which the seed is planted and (4) the character of the lands selected for seeding. The U.S. Forest Service has experimented with the comparative suitability of some 15 of the most promising kinds of grasses and clovers in attempting to reseed various overgrazed Forest ranges including the Great Basin Experimental Range. The time in the year seeds are scattered appears to have a good deal to do with the stand obtained, the vigor of the plants, and their ability to withstand drought during the first year of growth. Autumn is the most satisfactory time to sow, the spring coming second, summer third, while winter is the least satisfactory. The reason why fall seeding gives better

USDA Forest Service Gen. Tech. Rep. RMRS-GTR-305WWW. 2013

75

results than sowing in the spring is that a much better root system is developed. Observations and research on the Great Basin Experimental Range contributed to the conclusions presented in this report.

156. Sampson, Arthur W. 1916. The brome grasses. National Wool Grower 6(3): 38-40.

There are on record about 100 different kinds of brome grasses. Of this number, some 40 occur in the United States, about 30 of which are found on western ranges in varying abundance. The greater number is valuable on the range and some are of the highest value as forage plants. Eighteen brome grasses are emigrants from Europe; some of these are regarded by farmers as weed pests, while others are held in high esteem for grazing and for hay. On the whole, brome grasses are highly valuable on account of the fine quality of hay they produce and the relish with which they are cropped on the range, both when green and after maturity. Observations and research on the Great Basin Experimental Range contributed to the conclusions presented in this report.

157. Sampson, Arthur W. 1916. The fescue grasses. National Wool Grower 6(7): 17-19.

The fescues can best be distinguished from the grasses with which they are sometimes confused in that they have abruptly pointed glumes or chaff surrounding the seed, the lower glume of each seed being one-nerved and the upper three-nerved. The plants are either annuals, growing but a single year, or perennials. They are usually tufted or bunched in habit of growth. There are in all about 100 different kinds of fescue grasses, approximately forty kinds being found in North America and many of these occur on western ranges. Mountain fescue (*Festuca viridula*) is a high value, deeply rooted, perennial bunch grass with erect stems 1½ to 3 feet tall. Observations and research on the Great Basin Experimental Range contributed to the conclusions presented in this report.

158. Sampson, Arthur W. 1916. Poisonous range plants. National Wool Grower 6(12): 25-27.

The importance of proper herding and adequate salting are the keys to the prevention of serious poisoning. Probably 90 per cent of the heavy sheep losses from poison occur when the animals are ravenously hungry following long drives or staying too long in one place. Again, if the animals are supplied with ample salt at all times their systems seem to be able to throw off the effect of poison much better than if the animals are salt hungry. Suitable salt troughs are, therefore, an important consideration. Poison is usually considered any substance when taken internally that acts in a noxious manner other than mechanical, either causing death or interfering more or less seriously with health. The specific alkaloids and other agents found in different poisonous plants vary widely both in their toxic effect on the animal and in their chemical and physical properties. Observations and research on the Great Basin Experimental Range contributed to the conclusions presented in this report.

USDA Forest Service Gen. Tech. Rep. RMRS-GTR-305WWW. 2013

76

159. Sampson, Arthur W. 1916. The stability of aspen as a type. Proceedings of the Society of American Foresters 11(1): 86-87.

Aspen is believed to be a temporary forest type that will be slowly but surely replaced by conifers. It has been repeatedly observed that while conifers can invade aspen, the aspen cannot invade conifer stands. Data is presented showing that subalpine fir in an aspen dominated stand grows much faster, nearly six times based on diameter growth, than aspen does. Observations and research on the Great Basin Experimental Range contributed to the conclusions presented in this report.

160. Sampson, Arthur W. 1917. Important range plants: their live history and forage value. Bulletin 545. Washington, DC: U.S. Department of Agriculture. 63 p.

It is a well-established fact that the amount of moisture remaining in the soil when the plant wilts beyond recovery is determined by the physical structure of the substratum. The object in making the wilting coefficient determinations, then, is principally to show (1) that certain species occupy quite different soil types, and (2) that the soil types (textures) are widely contrasted as shown by the notable difference in the wilting coefficients for the various species. For example, mountain bunchgrass (*Festuca viridula*) does not wilt seriously in the soil in which it characteristically grows until the water content is reduced to between 7 and 9.5 percent. This plant is adapted to coarser and less rich soils than is mountain onion (*Allium validum*), for example, which is confined to exceptionally black, mealy soils, and which wilts beyond recovery when the soil moisture content drops to between 14 and 16 percent. Owing to the relatively small amount of moist soil found in mountain rangelands, it is evident that a species like mountain onion would not occur nearly as abundantly as mountain bunch grass. As a means of comparing habitat requirements, the species are grouped in three classes: Class A, plants of high moisture requirement—those inhabiting saturated soils, such as open marshes, wet meadows and bogs; Class B, plants of medium moisture requirement—those inhabiting relatively heavy soils that are saturated during the early part of the season, but later contain a medium amount of moisture; and Class C, plants of low moisture requirement—those occurring in well-drained lands, open glades, and exposed situations. It will be observed that practically three-fourths of the most valuable forage species are dry-land plants. This fact is of high economic importance, since the major portion of the rangelands are well drained and afford conditions favorable only to plants that are comparatively drought resistant. It is noted that a few species fall under more than one head so far as concerns their habitat requirements—that is, they are not strictly confined to any one soil type. Such plants, however, do not afford nearly the amount of forage those do that are found generally in the more open habitat (usually referred to as drought-resistant plants) where the soil is not finely disintegrated, is less well supplied with organic material, and has a wilting coefficient notably lower. A relatively small proportion of the rangelands are wet throughout the growing season, while bogs, marshes, and the like almost invariably support a more luxuriant stand of vegetation than any other, the herbage usually lacks in two essentials—palatability and nutritiousness. Those who have observed stock as to their choice of forage have noticed that sheep avoid marshes and wet habitats to a marked degree, cattle drift to the better drained lands for most of their feed, and horses, if unaccustomed to marsh vegetation, such, for example, as sedges and rushes, graze it eagerly for a couple of days, after which they will not remain on the succulent feed if any other is available. Campers and mountain workers have found that their pack and saddle animals cannot do the work when feeding on marsh and bog vegetation that they can on drier feed. Also, stockmen have found that fat made on succulent feeds is not of a solid character and in the case of long drives to market or of shipment shrinkage is abnormally heavy. Observations and research on the Great Basin Experimental Range contributed to the conclusions presented in this report.

161. Sampson, Arthur W. 1917. Succession as a factor in range management. Journal of Forestry 15(5): 593-596.

By succession is meant the establishment of plant species by a series of invasions in a given habitat causing the replacement of one set of plants by another. This alternation in the vegetative personnel is apparent when the natural conditions of the habitat have been disturbed either by physical or biotic forces. Where the vegetative cover has been interfered with more or less seriously, as is often the case on pasture and range lands, but where subsequently these disturbances have been eliminated or decreased in intensity, there is a tendency through successive invasions, for the vegetation gradually to become more like the original. The succession continues until the equilibrium is finally established between the environment and the vegetation that it supports. This vegetative state marks the ultimate, climax, or stable type and is quite in harmony with the world around. In general the stability of the vegetation cover of a pasture unit and the cropping of the herbage year after year are not particularly harmonious, though this will depend largely on the way in which the herbage is grazed. If, for instance, the leafage—the laboratory of the plant—is devoured each season at a time when the elaborated food material is needed for the proper development of the vegetation and for seed production, the effect of grazing may be reflected in various ways: (1) delay in the time at which growth begins in the spring; (2) decreased size and number of leaves; (3) fewer flower stalks coupled with later appearance of the stalks; (4) delayed seed maturity, limited seed production, and lowered vitality of the seed crop; and (5) low germination and limited establishment of seedling plants in the following spring. Hence the stability of the type is interfered with and the invasion and succession of transitory species made possible. Observations and research on the Great Basin Experimental Range contributed to the conclusions presented in this report.

162. Sampson, Arthur W. 1918. Climate and plant growth in certain vegetative associations. Bulletin 700. Washington, DC: U.S. Department of Agriculture. 72 p.

The investigation reported here was conducted in the vicinity of the Great Basin Experimental Range located on the Wasatch Plateau on the Manti National Forest in central Utah. Here, from the foothills to the highest elevations, between altitudes of approximately 7,000 and 11,000 feet, four distinct plant associations occur. In the heart of each of these associations a type station was selected in 1913.

USDA Forest Service Gen. Tech. Rep. RMRS-GTR-305WWW. 2013

78

From 1913 to 1916 the more important environmental factors were recorded, and accordingly the climatic characteristics of each type are well known. The types recognized and their approximate altitudinal limits are sagebrush-rabbitbrush association, 5,200—6,500 feet; oak brush association, 6,500—7,800 feet; aspen-fir association, 7,500—9,500 feet; spruce-fir association, 9,000—11,000 feet. The investigations have been concerned chiefly with (1) recording and summarizing the meteorological data, and (2) determining the relation of certain potent weather factors to growth, water requirement, and certain other physiological functions of standard plants developed under different climatic conditions. Measurements of growth and certain other activities were recorded from time to time throughout the season. The plants used in each station were a pedigreed strain of Canadian field pea (*Pisum arvense*) known as the Kaiser variety, cultivated wheat (*Triticum durum*) known as Kubanka No. 1440, and mountain brome grass (*Bromus marginatus*) native to the Rocky Mountains. From the study here reported, it may be concluded that in this locality Kubanka wheat and Canadian field peas, and doubtless other agricultural crops, cannot be grown profitably at elevations exceeding about 8,000 feet because of the lack of sufficient heat. Native forage plants are of high value in the pasturing of livestock in contrast to the failure of agricultural plants.

163. Sampson, Arthur W. 1918. The Great Basin Experiment Station. National Wool Grower 8(4): 19-21.

While there are six Forest Experiment Stations in existence, all of which are located in the West, the Great Basin Station (Great Basin Experimental Range) in central Utah is an innovation in that it is the only one that represents the extensive grazing interests on our national forests. The Great Basin Experiment Station, the main building site of which is nestled in the rugged mountains at an elevation of 8,700 feet, is located on the Manti National Forest, 8 miles (on an airline) east of Ephraim, Utah, in the heart of a great livestock region. Principal research activities of the Station will be poison plant eradication, natural reseeding, plants as indicators of range conditions, and management of eroded lands.

164. Sampson, Arthur W. 1919. Effect of grazing upon aspen reproduction. Bulletin No. 741. Washington, DC: U.S. Department of Agriculture. 29 p.

Aspen, a tree of high commercial value on many national forests in the West, and on some of the farm woodlots and lands adjacent there to in the northeastern United States, is often reproduced with difficulty where the lands are made to serve the double purpose of timber and meat production. The leafage, young twigs, and branches of the reproduction are browsed with varying degrees of relish by both cattle and sheep. Sheep are responsible for severe damage to the reproduction, both as it occurs in standing timber and on clear cuttings. Cattle cause less damage. The injury and mortality chargeable to the presence of livestock is roughly proportional to the closeness to which the lands are grazed. On clear-cut lands, where the reproduction is conspicuous and the stand even, the annual mortality due to sheep grazing is exceedingly heavy. Only slight difference is recorded in extent and character of browsing either by sheep or by cattle on different height classes of reproduction, so long as the total height growth of the sprouts has not passed the limit at which stock find the food accessible. In lands protected from grazing, aspen sprouts are produced only during the first two seasons after cutting. On grazed lands a considerable number of sprouts are sent up for three successive seasons following the removal of the timber. When logging is done on sheep range, or on a combination sheep and cattle range, the forthcoming reproduction will be destroyed almost to the last sprout if the areas are even moderately grazed by sheep during the first 3 years following the cutting. To avoid destruction of the young aspen cover, only three courses are open: (1) entire exclusion of grazing for three successive seasons following logging, (2) exceedingly light grazing by sheep, and (3) moderate grazing by cattle. Observations and research on the Great Basin Experimental Range contributed to the conclusions presented in this report.

165. Sampson, Arthur W. 1919. Plant succession in relation to range management. Bulletin No. 791. Washington, DC: U.S. Department of Agriculture. 76 p.

The carrying capacity of a large portion of the millions of acres of western ranges has been materially decreased as a result of too early grazing, overstocking, and other faulty management. One of the most serious handicaps has been the lack of means of recognizing overgrazing in its early or incipient stages, which has carried with it inability to correct the factor causing the damage before the carrying capacity of the range was more or less seriously depleted. In deciding upon the lands especially in need of improvement in the past, stockmen and forest officers regulating grazing have relied chiefly on the general abundance and luxuriance of the forage supply and on the condition of the stock grazed. By these general observations, however, it is not possible to recognize overgrazing before a large proportion of the plants have been killed. The most rational and reliable way of recognizing the incipient destruction of the forage supply is to note the replacement of one type of plant cover by another, a phenomenon that is usually much in evidence on lands used for the grazing of livestock. In tracing the succession of plant life from the consolidated rock to a well-disintegrated, fertile soil several fairly distinct cover stages are recognized. These stages may be grouped as follows: (1) the algae-lichen type, the pioneer stage; (2) the lichen-moss type with its sparse stand of annual herbs, the transition stage; (3) the ruderal-weed type of cover of annual plants with a scattered stands of short-lived perennials, the first weed stage; (4) perennial herbs, chiefly weeds, the second-weed stage; and (5) the long-lived perennial grasses, known as the subclimax, or under some conditions, the climax type. In order to observe the principles of succession in the building up as well as in the deterioration of the range, special studies were initiated on the high summer range of the Wasatch Plateau in central Utah. After a careful survey of the vegetation, four major consociations were recognized, namely, the wheatgrass, the porcupine-grass-yellow brush, the foxglove-sweet sage-yarrow, and the ruderal, early weed. The data in this bulletin justify the conclusion that the character of the native vegetation can be used as a reliable indicator of the condition of the range and of the effect of a given method of grazing of the plant cover. Observations and research on the Great Basin Experimental Range contributed to the conclusions presented in this report.

USDA Forest Service Gen. Tech. Rep. RMRS-GTR-305WWW. 2013

80

166. Sampson, Arthur W. 1919. Suggestions for instruction in range management. Journal of Forestry 17(5): 523-545.

The advancement in forestry methods in this country during the past decade is very marked. That forest schools are deserving of much credit for this advancement requires no argument. However, one highly important phase of forestry business, namely, range and livestock management, has, up to the present time been all but overlooked. When one stops to consider that there is no other single activity on the national forests that exercises so profound and immediate an influence on the people of the communities adjacent to the forests as does range and livestock management, it is truly amazing that a thorough, ongoing course in this field of activity has not long since been included in the curricula of the leading forest schools. With the right balance in foundational training and with well-balanced technical courses, the range technician as well as the technical forester should prove his worth both in public and private work. Observations and research on the Great Basin Experimental Range contributed to the conclusions presented in this report.

167. Sampson, Arthur W. 1920. Herding hints from the changing range. National Wool Grower 10(5): 21-22.

In this study two 10-acre areas on the Great Basin Experimental Range were selected having similar slope, exposure, and soil, but differing appreciably in the density of plant cover. On the area where the plant cover had been well opened up by destructive grazing as much as 50,000 pounds of air dry sediment has on several occasions been carried down by a single heavy rainstorm. The other area that had better cover was grazed in the same manner eroded but little. Careful soil tests have clearly shown that the plant nutrients in the soil are roughly in proportion to the extent of destruction of the vegetation and the degree of the erosion, the soil least eroded, of course, being the most fertile. Among other things, the soil tests show that the non-eroded soil contains an average of approximately four times more total organic matter, three times more total nitrogen, and several other elements of fertility in proportion, than eroded soil. Repeated use year after year of established bedgrounds and stock driveways provide examples of the higher destruction and more desirable types of plant life. For better conservation, these practices need to be modified.

168. Sampson, Arthur W. 1923. Our native broad-leaved forage plants. National Wool Grower 13(5); 17-19; 13(6): 15-17; 13(7): 25-28; 13(9): 28-31.

This series of review articles draws, in part, from the author's experiences at the Great Basin Station (Great Basin Experimental Range) and includes anecdotal experiences from that location as well as others. The use, distribution, and habitat of both forbs (herbaceous broad-leaved plants) and shrubs (woody broad-leaved plants) are reviewed. Important forbs from the borage, bunchflower, carrot, evening primrose, geranium, pea, sunflower, and valerian families are described and illustrated. For shrubs, the families thus treated are the buckthorn, heath, oak, rose, sunflower, and willow families.

USDA Forest Service Gen. Tech. Rep. RMRS-GTR-305WWW. 2013

81

169. Sampson, Arthur W. 1923. Range and pasture management. New York: John Wiley & Sons, Inc. 421 p.

This textbook draws in part from the author's experience at the Great Basin Station (Great Basin Experimental Range) and is divided into four parts. Part I, the grazing industry and range control includes chapters on the pasture lands and grazing control in the United States; national forest, State, and private grazing lands. Part II, pasture revegetation and forage maintenance presents chapters on reseeding western grazing lands to cultivated forage plants, natural reseeding and maintenance of native western pasture lands, improvement and management of farm pastures, recognizing and correcting declining forage yield, principal introduced forage grasses, and principal introduced non-grass-like forage herbs. Part III, range and pasture protection has chapters on the control of erosion on range and pasture, grazing on woodlands and its relation to the future timber supply, burning of pasture lands and its effects on forage production, stock-poisoning plants and their control, principal stock-poisoning plants, and poisonous and mechanically injurious plants of secondary or local importance. Part IV, pasture improvements and research methods chapters present information on the development of watering places for range and pasture stock, forage estimates as a basis for the rational use of grazing resources (grazing reconnaissance), grazing capacity and pasture inspection, research methods in range and pasture revegetation, and suggestions for instruction in pasture management and livestock production.

170. Sampson, Arthur W. 1924. Native American forage plants. New York: John Wiley & Sons, Inc. 435 p.

This textbook draws in part from the author's experience at the Great Basin Station (Great Basin Experimental Range) and is divided into two parts. Part I, plant life of the pasture includes pasture forage and animal nutrition; how plants live, grow, and reproduce (applied plant physiology); environment of range and pasture plants and forces that influence them (applied plant ecology); classification, collection, and preservation of plant specimens (applied taxonomic botany). Part Two, important native forage plants—"all flesh is grass" presents information about important native forage grasses and the characters that describe them; wheatgrasses and barley-grasses (*Hordeae*); fescues, bluegrasses, and bromegrasses (*Festuceae*); oatgrasses (*Avenae*) and gramagrasses and buffalograss (*Chlorideae*); redtops, timothies, and needlegrasses (*Agrostideae*) and miscellaneous species; comparative forage-value classification of native pasture grasses; grasslike forage plants; leaves, flowers, and fruit of broad-leaved forage plants and the characters that describe them; plants of the pea and carrot families; plants of the sunflower, borage, and honeysuckle families; plants of the buttercup, rose, willow, buckthorn, figwort, huckleberry, and valerian families; plants of the goosefoot, beech, geranium, gooseberry, mallow, bunchflower, evening primrose, and apple families; comparative forage-value, classification of important genera of broad-leaved plants.

171. Sampson, Arthur W. 1928. Livestock husbandry on range and pasture. New York: John Wiley & Sons, Inc. 411 p.

USDA Forest Service Gen. Tech. Rep. RMRS-GTR-305WWW. 2013

82

This textbook draws in part from the author's experience at the Great Basin Station (Great Basin Experimental Range) and is divided into four parts. Part I, range history and livestock improvement provides information about the livestock industry, meat consumption, and prospective meat supply; and practical methods of improving domestic foraging animals. Part II, pasture husbandry of sheep and goats—leading breeds of fine-wooled and coarse-wooled sheep: discusses their adaptability to range and farm; leading breeds of medium-wooled sheep: their adaptability range and farm; judging the qualities of sheep; livestock handling in relation to seasonal plans of pasture use; raising sheep on the range: camp tending, herding, bedding, watering, and salting; raising sheep on the range: breeding, lambing, and docking; raising sheep on the farm; the wool crop and the wool grower; common diseases of sheep and their control; raising goats on the range and farm. Part III, pasture husbandry of beef cattle—leading breeds of beef cattle: discusses their adaptability to range and farm; judging the qualities of beef cattle; raising cattle on the range: the breeding herd, breeding practices, production of calves; raising cattle on the range: general handling, winter husbandry; raising cattle on the farm; common diseases of cattle and their control. Part IV, economics of pasture livestock—cost accounting and budgeting in livestock production; includes information about animals that prey on livestock and rodents that destroy forage crops; wild animal life and recreation areas: their relation to livestock production; reindeer production as a range industry.

172. Sampson, Arthur, W; Malmsten, Harry E. 1926. Grazing periods and forage production on the National Forests. Bulletin 1405. Washington, DC: U.S. Department of Agriculture. 55 p.

To maintain the forage productivity of the range it is necessary to be able to determine (1) when the range is ready for grazing, (2) the intensity and frequency of grazing that may be allowed, (3) how to handle the stock, and (4) the natural revegetation of the range that may be relied on. Observations at the Great Basin Experimental Range indicate that the season of grazing should close when proper utilization of the old growth has been obtained and soon enough for the forage plants to make satisfactory new growth. The grazing seasons giving the best results in the central Wasatch region are: oakbrush, May 20 to June 9 and October 1 to October 15; aspen-fir, June 10 to July 9 and October 1 to October 15; and spruce-fir, July 10 to September 30. To insure proper seasonal use, a thoroughly sound and practical grazing-management plan should be developed in accordance with the growth and development of the feed. Sheep, being under herding, can readily be confined to seasonal zones during the best period for use. Cattle ranges should be divided into distribution units so as to make practicable the control of the stock. The control, distribution, and movement of the number of cattle that can use each unit to best advantage is obtained by salting in accordance with definite plans, by riding, by drift fences, or by a combination of two or all of these. Improvement and maintenance of native pasture lands, the forage of which is composed largely of bunch grasses, is dependent on the periodical production of a fertile seed crop. Seed production of the more palatable forage plants is enhanced by avoiding early grazing and overgrazing, and effective control and distribution of stock. Deferred and rotation grazing, which imply the withholding of part of the range from grazing until after seed maturity each year, have given conspicuous results in range reseeding. Experiments showed that range revegetation is accomplished by deferred grazing almost as well as protection yearlong from foraging animals.

173. Sampson, Arthur W.; Weyl, Leon H. 1918. Range preservation and its relation to erosion control on western grazing lands. Bulletin 675. Washington, DC: U.S. Department of Agriculture. 35 p.

The maintenance of an effective vegetative cover may be accomplished by the following means: (1) avoidance of overgrazing; (2) avoidance of too early grazing; (3) deferred and rotation grazing; (4) artificial reseeding (in choice sites only); (5) proper control and distribution of stock. Where the depletion of the soil and the formation of long established gullies make thorough revegetation impossible, destructive floods and erosion may be controlled in the following ways: (1) total exclusion of stock; (2) terracing and planting; (3) construction of dams. Erratic run-off and erosion have been responsible for a great deal of damage on western ranges where the vegetative cover had previously been materially decreased or practically eliminated. Though the damage from erosion usually is measured merely by the injury caused to farmland and works of construction, the damage to the forest rangelands on which erosion occurs is often greater and shows itself in a decrease in carrying capacity of the lands. While topography, climate, and soil are the primary factors in determining erosion, the combination of these factors on the lands under consideration is such that erosion is slight where the native ground cover has not been greatly disturbed. The seriousness of the erosion, therefore, is largely determined by the extent to which the ground cover is maintained. Serious erosion on western rangelands is due chiefly to the destruction of the vegetation as a result of overgrazing and mismanagement of livestock. The sum of conditions favoring destructive run-off and erosion is most pronounced in the fan-shaped drainage basins of the spruce fir type (on the Great Basin Experimental Range of the Manti National Forest between 9,000 and 10,500 feet), where the ground cover is naturally rather sparse, where there is a characteristic sparseness of tree growth, and where the most desirable summer sheep ranges are located. To maintain an effective vegetative cover, overgrazing and too early cropping of the herbage must be avoided, deferred and rotation grazing should be applied, and stock should be properly controlled and distributed at all times in the season. In the case of incipient erosion, only slight changes in the use of the lands are generally necessary, and these changes do not necessarily imply even a temporary financial loss. Where erosion has had full play for a number of years, the reestablishment of the ground cover, even though grazing is discontinued, does not always afford adequate protection. In such instances, which fortunately are relatively rare in this country, a combination of terracing and planting or, in exceptional cases, the construction of dams is justified.

USDA Forest Service Gen. Tech. Rep. RMRS-GTR-305WWW. 2013

84

174. Stevens, Richard. 2003. Historical summary: oldest watershed study in America, Wasatch Plateau, Utah, Great Basin Experiment Station. In: Keammerer, Warren R.; Redente, Edward F., editors. Proceedings of the 15th high altitude revegetation workshop; 2002 March 6-8; Fort Collins: CO. Information Series No. 95. Fort Collins, CO: Colorado Water Resources Research Institute, Colorado State University: 94-100.

Starting in 1912, Watersheds A and B, two adjoining depleted subalpine watersheds on the Great Basin Experimental Range at the head of Ephraim Canyon, Utah, have been under continuous study. Since 1920 Watershed A has been protected from grazing. This protection resulted in a rapid increase in plant cover, especially forbs, on all but the more depleted areas. Increase in plant cover has resulted in substantial reduction in runoff and sedimentation. On Watershed B, heavy grazing reduced ground cover and changed a fairly stable watershed to a serious flood-source area. Immediate control of summer runoff and sedimentation was achieved with disking, contour trenching, and seeding of grasses and leguminous forbs in 1952. Watershed stabilization can be much more rapidly accomplished using restoration techniques than long periods of nonuse.

175. Stevens, Richard; McArthur, E. Durant; Davis, James N. 1992. Reevaluation of vegetative cover changes, erosion, and sedimentation on two watersheds—1912-1983. In: Clary, Warren P.; McArthur, E. Durant; Bedunah, Don; Wambolt, Carl L., comps. Proceedings—symposium on ecology and management of riparian shrub communities; 1991 May 29-31; Sun Valley, ID. Gen. Tech. Rep. INT-289. Ogden, UT: U.S. Department of Agriculture, Forest Service, Intermountain Research Station: 123-128.

Watersheds A and B, on two adjoining, depleted subalpine watersheds in the Great Basin Experimental Range at the head of Ephraim Canyon, Utah, have been under continuous study since 1912. Watershed A has been protected from grazing since 1920. This protection resulted in a rapid increase in plant cover on all but the more depleted areas. Although Watershed A is still in marginal condition, increase in plant cover has resulted in substantial reduction in runoff and sedimentation. In Watershed B, heavy grazing reduced ground cover and changed a fairly stable watershed to a serious flood-source area. Immediate control of summer runoff and sedimentation was achieved with disking, contour trenching, and seeding of grasses and leguminous forbs. Watershed B would now support controlled livestock use without producing runoff and erosion. Watershed stabilization can be much more rapidly accomplished using restoration techniques than long periods of nonuse. Both systems have a place, depending on the urgency of restoration and management objectives.

176. Stevens, Richard; Plummer, A. Perry; Jensen, Chester E.; Giunta, Bruce C. 1974. Site productivity classification for selected species on winter big game ranges of Utah. Res. Pap. INT-158. Ogden, UT: U.S. Department of Agriculture, Forest Service, Intermountain Forest and Range Experiment Station. 24 p.

USDA Forest Service Gen. Tech. Rep. RMRS-GTR-305WWW. 2013

85

Productivity of a mixture of four range grasses and big and black sagebrush was correlated with soil characteristics, topography, and precipitation at 21 sites considered representative of Utah's juniper-piñion and sagebrush-grass types. The mathematical models developed provide site evaluation guides for use in range improvement programs. Charts give productivity potential in five broad groups. This research was performed, in part, on the Great Basin Experimental Range.

177. Stewart, George. 1940. Forest Service range research seminar. Journal of the American Society of Agronomy 32(3): 235-238.

In keeping with on-coming expansion in demand for adequate information regarding range forage and rangeland use and management, a conference of major interest was help July 10-22, 1939, at the Great Basin Branch of the Intermountain Forest and Range Experiment Station (Great Basin Experimental Range), near Ephraim, Utah, by the U.S. Forest Service, to take stock of objectives, plans, procedures, and techniques applicable to range research problems. The problems most carefully analyzed at the conference were those dealing with (1) the development of sound research programs based on regional and local problem analysis; (2) research methodology, including experimental design and statistical analysis; and (3) vegetation problems such as forage growth and production, vegetative changes, trends and conditions, utilization of the forage crop and artificial revegetation. Problems dealing with multiple rangeland uses, handling livestock on the range and animal nutrition were also included, as well as those pertaining to publications, recruiting personnel, cooperation with other research agencies, and the need for, and the means of accomplishing intelligent range extension education.

178. Stewart, George. 1945. Range reseeding and grazing use of reseeded lands in Utah. Proceedings of the Utah Academy of Sciences, Arts and Letters 22:10.

Two organized experimental tests are now under way: one at the Great Basin Experimental Range near Ephraim, Utah, where a crested wheatgrass field is being grazed by sheep, at three intensities and beginning at two different dates; and a second at Benmore, Utah, where 100-acre pastures of crested wheatgrass are being grazed by cattle, also testing the time and intensity of spring grazing. The first experiment is being conducted by the Intermountain Forest and Range Experiment Station and the second by a four-way cooperation of the Soil Conservation Service, the Utah Experiment Station, the Bureau of Plant Industry, and the Intermountain Forest and Range Experiment Station. Both of these gazing experiments, if continued to completion, will yield valuable data and will be watched by all who are interested in this phase of agriculture.

179. Stewart, George. 1947. Increasing forage by range reseeding. National Wool Grower 37(1): 17-19.

Forage produced after reseeding, whether measured by the amount of forage grown or in sheep months of grazing obtained, has been in most case from 5 to 15 times as great as the same ranges before reseeding. This was the case in comparisons between reseeded range and adjacent similar range not seeded at sites in

Utah—near Ephraim, in Cedar Valley near Fairfield, and on Lost Creek near Richfield; in Idaho—near Dubois, on Raft River, and on Willow Creek about 35 miles southeast of Boise; and in Ruby Valley, Nevada. This research was performed, in part, at the Great Basin Experimental Range.

180. Stewart, George. 1949. Range reseeding by airplane compared with standard ground methods. Agronomy Journal 41(7): 283-288.

On most rangelands, reseeding by standard on-the-ground procedures developed from careful research has so far given much more dependable results than has airplane seeding, both in getting a stand and in obtaining good yields of forage. The yields from airplane seeding on sagebrush ranges have been found to be from 50 to 150 pounds of air-dry forage per acre. On similar areas the yields obtained by recommended ground procedures have been from 300 to 3,000 pounds of air-dry herbage, an amount 5 to 50 times as much as from airplane seeding. To insure successful growth of reseeded species in the arid western United States, all seeds need to be covered to a shallow, uniform depth. Seeding of rangelands by airplane is still in its exploratory stages, and undoubtedly many improvements in methods and techniques will be developed. Observations and research on the Great Basin Experimental Range contributed to the conclusions presented in this report.

181. Stewart, George; Forsling, C. L. 1931. Surface runoff and erosion in relation to soil and plant cover on high grazing lands of central Utah. Journal of the American Society of Agronomy. 23: 815-832.

On the elevated grazing lands of the Great Basin Experimental Range of central Utah, surface run-off and the sediment carried have been studied since 1915. Two nearby experimental watersheds of approximately equal area, at an elevation of about 10,000 feet, and so located and equipped as to permit the measurement of the precipitation, the run-off water, and the sediment carried, differed widely in their plant cover. Roughly, 3 to 5 times as much total water ran off the area with the poorer plant cover.

182. Stewart, George; Plummer, A. Perry. 1947. Reseeding range lands by airplane in Utah. Proceedings of the Utah Academy of Sciences, Arts, and Letters 24: 35-39.

The rapidity of seeding by airplane, its comparatively low cost, the possibility of easily distributing seeds on areas with rough topography, and the lure of doing things in a spectacular manner have all aided in arousing considerable interest in the possibility of airplane seeding. There has been a strong demand for information on this subject. To meet this demand an investigation was planned to study the feasibility of using an airplane for rangeland reseeding. In September 1946, data were taken on the areas seeded by airplane on October 2-9, 1945, to determine how much of a stand had been obtained. Data were taken on 156 plots of 10 square feet each in meandering transects of three areas. No young plants were found on 61 plots. On the other plots the number of plants varied from less than 10 to more than 60 per plot. When the plots with no seedlings were included, the average number of 0.89

USDA Forest Service Gen. Tech. Rep. RMRS-GTR-305WWW. 2013

87

and 0.75 per square foot in the two aspen areas and 0.74 per square foot in the oakbrush area were obtained. Past experience has shown that a considerable part of the seeds broadcast by hand in similar conditions germinates in the second season as is borne out by the data collected in 1947. Of 298 plots used to sample the area in 1947, all except 29 included seeding plants, raising the average up to 1.09 plants per square foot in aspen and 0.90 in the oakbrush. The present number of around one plant per square foot will produce a fair to good stand of mature grass without further germination and further germination is expected so that the stand outlook is better than one plant per square foot. Observations and research on the Great Basin Experimental Range contributed to the conclusions presented in this report.

183. Stewart, George; Walker, R. H.; Price, Raymond. 1939. Reseeding range lands of the Intermountain region. Farmers' Bulletin No. 1823. Washington, DC: U.S. Department of Agriculture. 25 p.

Revegetating deteriorated rangelands by sowing adaptable, nutritious, and palatable grasses is vital for adequate forage production in the Intermountain region, for profitable livestock raising, and as a safeguard against flood and erosion damage. The effect of serious droughts, greatly aggravated by overstocking, has resulted in the replacement of valuable perennial grasses by annual weeds and grasses that have much less value as forage for livestock or for proper soil protection. The abandonment of unsuccessful submarginal croplands has also added greatly to the vast acreage of deteriorated but potentially productive rangelands of the region in need of revegetation. Proper guides and procedures for revegetating degraded ranges and abandoned dry farms by artificial reseeding are necessary to safeguard against costly pitfalls and to insure reasonable success. The procedures herein outlined are based on the experiences and research to date and should prove helpful to those administering rangelands and producing livestock in the region comprising Utah, Nevada, southern Idaho, and southwestern Wyoming, commonly referred to the Intermountain region. Observations and research on the Great Basin Experimental Range contributed to the conclusions presented in this report.

184. Tew, Ronald K. 1967. Soil moisture depletion by aspen in central Utah. Res. Note INT-73. Ogden, UT: U.S. Department of Agriculture, Forest Service, Intermountain Forest and Range Experiment Station. 8 p.

Aspect and elevation of site and age of vegetation affect the amount of soil moisture depleted by aspen (*Populus tremuloides* Michx.) during the growing season at the Great Basin Experimental Range in central Utah. Clones on west aspects used more soil moisture than those on either north- or south-facing slopes. Differences in elevation had little effect on the amount of soil moisture depleted by mature aspen, but sprout stands used significantly greater amounts of soil moisture on the lower elevation sites. As much as 5 inches of moisture was conserved in the upper 6 feet of soil during the first season after aspen removal, but as sprout stand became reestablished, there was a decrease in these moisture savings.

185. Tew, Ronald K. 1967. Soil moisture depletion by Gambel oak in central Utah. Res. Note INT-74. Ogden, UT: U.S. Department of Agriculture, Forest Service, Intermountain Forest and Range Experiment Station. 7 p.

Aspect and elevation of site and age of vegetation affect the amount of soil moisture depleted by Gambel oak (*Quercus gambelii* Nutt.) during the growing season at the Great Basin Experimental Range in central Utah. More soil moisture was lost at the higher elevation (7,900 feet) than at the lower (6,600 feet) on all aspects. A south-facing site at the higher elevation lost the most moisture, whereas one at the lower elevation lost the least. Most available soil moisture was depleted to a depth of 6 feet on all sites during seasons of normal rainfall. Removing oak and allowing regrowth of a vigorous sprout stand reduced soil moisture depletion nearly an inch during the year following cutting, but by the end of the third year, sprout stands were using up to an inch more soil moisture that mature stands.

186. Tippets, David; Anderson, Val Jo. 1991. Partnership preserves historic range research sites. Rangelands 13(3): 121-124.

A team of 109 volunteer workers from government agencies, universities, and other Institutions combined forces at the Great Basin Experimental Range east of Ephraim, Utah, on July 13-14, 1990, to preserve some of the oldest range research sites in the world. Starting in 1912, pioneer range ecologist Arthur W. Sampson built log exclosure fences to protect his study plots from domestic livestock grazing. After 78 years of deep snow and decay, Sampson's fences had decayed to the point livestock could step across them and graze the study sites. Grazing study sites that had been protected for 78 years would mean destroying a tremendous accumulation of data about natural succession without grazing impact. New grazing-enclosures, replacing old fences designed to protect permanently located study sites from sheep and cattle were installed by teams of six- to eight workers using the same primitive skills and tools used to construct the first protective barriers 78 years earlier.

187. U.S. Department of Agriculture, Forest Service. 1972. Auto tour Great Basin Experimental Range. GPO 781-170. Washington, DC: General Printing Office. 29 p.

This self-guiding tour provides assistance in exploring examples of research studies conducted and direction to points of interest along 10 miles over a 5,000-foot elevational gradient in the Great Basin Experimental Range.

188. Wagstaff, Fred J. 1983. Economic incentives for managing quaking aspen in the Mountain West and evaluating proposed improvements of public rangelands. Provo, UT: Brigham Young University. 40 p. Dissertation.

Thirty-one aspen stands in Ephraim Canyon, Utah were examined to determine to what degree conifer invasion was affecting the production of forage, wood fiber, and water. Data from these stands show clearly that conifer invasion reduces forage output and species diversity. When coupled with the results of other studies on water yield, the impact of conifer succession becomes clear. Values were assigned

USDA Forest Service Gen. Tech. Rep. RMRS-GTR-305WWW. 2013

89

to the forage, water, and wood fiber; and the benefit stream for each successional stage calculated on a present value basis. Allowing conifer to invade and dominate aspen sites reduced the present value by $147 per acre ($363/hectare). If all 4.5 million acres (2.5 million hectares) of aspen in the Rocky Mountains were allowed to become conifer, the loss would be $907 million. Observations and research on the Great Basin Experimental Range contributed to the conclusions presented in this report

189. Walker, Scott, C.; Mann, David K.; McArthur, E. Durant. 1996. Plant community changes over 54 years within the Great Basin Experimental Range, Manti-La Sal National Forest. In: Barrow, Jerry R.; McArthur, E. Durant; Sosebee, Ronald E.; Tausch, Robin J., comps. Proceedings: shrubland ecosystem dynamics in a changing environment; 1995 May 23-25; Las Cruces, NM. Gen. Tech. Rep. INT-GTR-338. Ogden, UT: U.S. Department of Agriculture, Forest Service, Intermountain Research Station: 66-68.

Plant community changes and natural succession over time impact forage values, watershed quality, wildlife habitat, and ecosystem dynamics. Comparisons were made between a vegetation map of community types completed in 1937 by the U.S. Forest Service, and vegetation maps compiled in 1990 of the same areas by satellite imagery, and through 1991 aerial photo interpretation combined with ground truthing. The study area includes nearly all of the drainage of the Great Basin Experimental Range in Ephraim Canyon located in central Utah, which consists of 6,027 acres (2,439 ha). Elevation ranges from 6,600 to 10,400 feet (2,040 to 3,210 m). Vegetation types ranged from pinyon-juniper woodland through oakbrush, mountain shrub, aspen, conifer and subalpine herbland. The comparison showed significant plant community changes and successional trends over the 54-year period.

190. Warner, James H.; Harper, K. T. 1972. Understory characteristics related to site-quality for aspen in Utah. Brigham Young University Science Bulletin Biological Series 16(2): 1-20.

An analysis has been made of the basic ecology of aspen forests of the mountainous areas of Utah and northern Arizona. Forty-nine study areas have been examined in respect to density, height and age of the tree cover, tree reproduction, and composition and biomass production of the understory. A graphic model of interspecific associations among prevalent understory species has been prepared by a cluster-analysis procedure based on presence and absence of species in 1,225 small quadrats (0.25 m^2) uniformly distributed among the 49 stands. The model separates species of relative stability as opposed to rapidly seral aspen forests. It also tends to separate species known to respond differently to grazing. An index for predicting site quality for aspen was devised using those species demonstrated to have indicator value. Sites having the best site quality for aspen also produce the greatest amount of understory forage. Prospects are good that the index can be refined to yield more precise estimates. Observations and research on the Great Basin Experimental Range contributed to the conclusions presented in this report.

USDA Forest Service Gen. Tech. Rep. RMRS-GTR-305WWW. 2013

90

191. Welch, Bruce L.; McArthur, E. Durant. 1979. Variation in winter levels of crude protein among *Artemisia tridentata* subspecies grown in a uniform garden. Journal of Range Management 32(6): 467-469.

The midwinter crude protein content of *Artemisia tridentata* is under genetic control. Some accessions of *A. tridentata* grown under uniform conditions contained significantly higher levels of crude protein than others. Subspecies *tridentata* contained significantly higher levels of crude protein than subspecies *vaseyana* and *wyomingensis*. The accessions that contained the highest levels of crude protein have been reported to be the least palatable to mule deer. A superior strain of *A. tridentata* can be developed by combining the high protein-yielding accessions with accessions that are higher in palatability. One of the subspecies *vaseyana* accessions in the study, Petty Bishop's Log, was from the Great Basin Experimental Range.

USDA Forest Service Gen. Tech. Rep. RMRS-GTR-305WWW. 2013

91

Chronological Index

1911 – 1919: 009, 010, 075, 151, 152, 153, 154, 155, 156, 157, 158, 159, 160, 161, 162, 163, 164, 165, 166, 173

1920 – 1929: 011, 012, 013, 015, 025, 052, 053, 054, 055, 090, 091, 092, 167, 168, 169, 170, 171, 172

1930 – 1939: 008, 014, 026, 031, 034, 035, 036, 056, 057, 058, 068, 104, 106, 115, 116, 149, 150, 181, 183

1940 – 1949: 006, 007, 027, 028, 032, 038, 039, 040, 041, 042, 043, 044, 049, 059, 062, 094, 105, 121, 122, 123, 124, 125, 139, 147, 177, 178, 179, 180, 182

1950 – 1959: 003, 020, 023, 033, 045, 046, 048, 050, 051, 060, 061, 063, 073, 074, 095, 096, 107, 119, 126, 136, 137, 138, 140, 141, 142, 143, 146

1960 – 1969: 021, 047, 076, 077, 078, 093, 108, 109, 120, 127, 128, 133, 134, 145, 184, 185,

1970 – 1979: 002, 016, 019, 022, 079, 080, 100, 110, 129, 130, 131, 132, 135, 144, 176, 187, 190, 191

1980 – 1989: 004, 029, 066, 067, 103, 111, 188

1990 – 1999: 005, 017, 018, 030, 064, 088, 089, 097, 101, 102, 114, 175, 186, 189

2000 – 2012: 001, 024, 037, 065, 069, 070, 071, 072, 081, 082, 083, 084, 085, 086, 087, 098, 099, 112, 113, 117, 118, 148, 174

Publication Type Index

Journal Article: 003, 006, 007, 009, 010, 011, 013, 015, 016, 017, 020, 021, 022, 023, 024, 025, 026, 027, 028, 029, 030, 032, 034, 035, 036, 038, 039, 040, 042, 043, 044, 045, 047, 048, 051, 052, 053, 054, 055, 057, 060, 061, 062, 063, 065, 068, 069, 078, 080, 088, 089, 090, 091, 094, 095, 096, 097, 100, 103, 106, 107, 108, 109, 115, 116, 121, 123, 124, 125, 126, 130, 137, 142, 150, 152, 153, 154, 155, 156, 157, 158, 159, 161, 163, 166, 167, 168, 177, 178, 179, 180, 181, 182, 186, 191

Book: 005, 064, 070, 081, 113, 117, 118, 169, 170, 171

Book Chapter: 044, 071, 082, 083, 084, 085, 086, 087, 127, 132

Symposium Proceedings: 033, 046, 066, 098, 102, 114, 131, 135, 144, 145, 174, 175, 189

Federal Agency Research Paper, Circular, Bulletin, leaflet, General Technical Report, Other Report: 001, 008, 012, 014, 018, 019, 031, 037, 049, 050, 056, 058, 072, 074, 075, 077, 079, 092, 093, 099, 101, 104, 105, 110, 111, 112, 119, 120, 122, 128, 129, 136, 138, 139, 147, 148, 149, 151, 160, 162, 164, 165, 172, 173, 176, 176, 183, 184, 185, 187

University Report: 190

State Agency Report: 133, 134, 140, 141, 143, 146

Dissertation (PhD): 041, 188

Thesis (MS): 002, 059, 067, 073, 076

Subject Matter Index

Community Ecology: 015, 021, 041, 045, 051, 093, 111, 162, 189

Disturbance (Grazing) Ecology: 044, 047, 048, 063, 075, 076, 088, 164

Fire Ecology: 024, 072

Historical and Site Description: 001, 004, 005, 064, 070, 071, 079, 080, 081, 082, 083, 084, 085, 086, 087, 097, 098, 099, 101, 102, 112, 117, 118, 148, 150, 163, 186, 187

Livestock Management: 052, 053, 055, 158, 167, 171

Mammal Ecology: 003

Methodology: 038, 062, 106, 107, 115, 116, 144, 180

Plant Autoecology: 002, 009, 012, 016, 029, 030, 073, 074, 137, 159, 188, 190

Plant Physiology: 010, 017, 020, 022, 061, 068, 078, 091, 104, 105, 191

Plant Taxonomy or Status: 011, 019, 103, 154, 156, 157, 160, 168

Range Ecology and Range Management: 007, 023, 028, 031, 039, 042, 046, 065, 114, 119, 121, 152, 153, 161, 165, 166, 169, 170, 172, 179

Research Needs Assessment: 025, 027, 037, 123, 177

Revegetation and Restoration Ecology: 018, 043, 058, 059, 060, 069, 092, 100, 113, 120, 122, 124, 125, 126, 127, 128, 129, 130, 131, 132, 133, 134, 135, 136, 138, 139, 140, 141, 142, 143, 145, 146, 147, 149, 155, 178, 182, 183

Site Evaluation and Species Performance: 014, 176

Soil Biology and Ecology: 013, 040, 089, 090, 184, 185

Watershed Ecology: 006, 008, 026, 032, 033, 034, 035, 036, 049, 050, 054, 056, 057, 066, 067, 077, 094, 095, 096, 108, 109, 110, 151, 173, 174, 175, 181

Author Index[5]

---

[5]Numbers refer to bibliographic entries; non-senior authorship is listed in parentheses.

USDA Forest Service Gen. Tech. Rep. RMRS-GTR-305WWW. 2013

93

Antrei A: 004, 005

Anderson, V: (186)

Bailey RW: 006, 007, 008, (050)

Baker FS: 009, 010, 011, 012, 013, 014, 015, (092)

Barnes BV: 016

Baskin CC: 017

Baskin JM: (017)

Blaisdell JP: (120)

Blauer AC: 018, 019

Bleak AT: 020, 021, 022, 023

Brown PM: 024, (072)

Campbell RB Jr.: (111)

Chapline WR: 025, 026, 027

Christensen DR: (133, 134, 135, 146)

Clark I: 028

Clary WP: 029, 030

Costello DF: 031

Craddock GW: 32, 33

Croft AR: 034, 035, 036, (049, 050)

Davis JN: 037, (175)

Dayton WA: (058)

Doty RD: (077)

Ellison L: 038, 039, 040, 041, 042, 043, 044, 045, 046, 047, 048, 049, 050, 051, (095)

Evans RB: (150)

Fenley JM: (136)

Fetherolf NJ: (015)

Forsling CL: 052, 053, 054, 055, 056, 057, 058 (181)

Freeman DC: (103)

Frischknecht NC: 059, 060, 061, 062, 063, (137)

Geary EA: 064

Gill RA: 065

Giunta BC: (019, 100, 176)

Godfrey AE: 066

Grah OJ: 067

Griswold SM: 068

Hall M: 069, 070, 071

Hancock NV: (135)

Harper KT: (190)

Heyerdahl, EK: (024), 072

Houston WR: (051), 073, 074

Hull AC Jr: (121, 138)

Hurd RM: (139)

Jardine JT: 075

Jensen CE: (176)

Jensen RL: (140, 141, 142, 143)

Johnson CM: (148)

Johnson HB: 076

Johnston RS: 077

Jorgensen KR: (144)

Julander O: 078

Keck WM: 079, 080

Kitchen SG: (024, 072)

Klade RJ: 081, 082, 083, 084, 085, 086, 087

Klemmendson JO: 088, 089

Korstian CF: 014, 015), 090, 091, 092

Laycock WA: 93

Loughry L: (1)

Lull, HW: 094, 095, 096

Malsten HE: (172)

Mann DK: (189)

Marston RB: (036)

McArthur ED: (018, 019), 097, 098, 099, 100, 101, 102, 103, (148, 175, 189, 191)

McCarty EC: 104, 105

McGinnies WG: 106

McGinnies WJ: 107

Meeuwig RO: 108, 109, 110

Meuggler, WF: 111

Meyer SE: (017)

Monsen SB: (101, 102), 112, 113, 114, (133, 134)

Nelson EW: 115, 116

Nelson SD: (018)

Norman LE: 117, 118

Orr HK: (096), 119

Parker KW: 120

Pearce CK: 121, 122, (139)

Pechanec JF: 123

Plaugher L: (1)

Plummer AP: (019, 023, 062, 063, 100, 122), 124,125, 126, 127, 128, 129, 130, 131, 132, 133, 134, 135, 136, 137, 138, 139, 140, 141, 142, 143, 144, 145, 146, 147, (176, 182)

Pope CL: (103)

Prevedel DA: 148

Price R: (031, 105), 149, 150, (183)

Reynolds RVR: 151

Robertson JH: (138)

Sampson A: 152, 153, 154, 155, 156. 157, 158, 159, 160, 161, 162, 163, 164, 165, 166, 167, 168, 169, 170, 171, 172, 173

Savage DA: (122)

Shaw NL: (113)

Stapley H: (141, 142, 143, 145, 146)

Stevens R: (018, 019, 102, 113, 114, 135), 174, 175, 176

Stewart G: (138, 147), 177, 178, 179, 180, 181, 182, 183

Tew RK: (077), 184, 185

Tiedemann AR: (029, 030, 088, 089)

Tippets D: 186

U. S. Department of Agriculture, Forest Service: 187

Wagstaff FJ: 188

Walker RH: (183)

Walker SC: (114), 189

Warner JH: 190

Weber MH: (024, 072)

Welch BL: 191

Weyl LH: (173)

Rocky Mountain Research Station

The Rocky Mountain Research Station develops scientific information and technology to improve management, protection, and use of the forests and rangelands. Research is designed to meet the needs of the National Forest managers, Federal and State agencies, public and private organizations, academic institutions, industry, and individuals. Studies accelerate solutions to problems involving ecosystems, range, forests, water, recreation, fire, resource inventory, land reclamation, community sustainability, forest engineering technology, multiple use economics, wildlife and fish habitat, and forest insects and diseases. Studies are conducted cooperatively, and applications may be found worldwide. For more information, please visit the RMRS web site at: www.fs.fed.us/rmrs.

Station Headquarters
Rocky Mountain Research Station
240 W Prospect Road
Fort Collins, CO 80526
(970) 498-1100

Research Locations

Flagstaff, Arizona	Reno, Nevada
Fort Collins, Colorado	Albuquerque, New Mexico
Boise, Idaho	Rapid City, South Dakota
Moscow, Idaho	Logan, Utah
Bozeman, Montana	Ogden, Utah
Missoula, Montana	Provo, Utah

To learn more about RMRS publications or search our online titles:

www.fs.fed.us/rm/publications

www.treesearch.fs.fed.us

USDA Forest Service Gen. Tech. Rep. RMRS-GTR-305WWW. 2013

98